THE BUTTERFLY CODE

D'YANNA CRAIGHEAD

THE BUTTERFLY CODE

LEARNING TO **SPREAD YOUR WINGS** THROUGH **PERSONAL EVOLUTION** AND **TRANSFORMATION**

Advantage | Books

Published by Advantage Books, Charleston, South Carolina.
An imprint of Advantage Media.

ADVANTAGE is a registered trademark, and the Advantage colophon is a trademark of Advantage Media Group, Inc.

Printed in the United States of America.

10 9 8 7 6 5 4 3 2 1

ISBN: 979-8-89188-077-1 (Hardcover)
ISBN: 979-8-89188-078-8 (eBook)

Library of Congress Control Number: 2024908746

Cover design by Matthew Morse.
Layout design by Ruthie Wood.

Advantage Books is an imprint of Advantage Media Group. Advantage Media helps busy entrepreneurs, CEOs, and leaders write and publish a book to grow their business and become the authority in their field. Advantage authors comprise an exclusive community of industry professionals, idea-makers, and thought leaders. For more information go to **advantagemedia.com**.

To Jaiden Simone.

Thank you for being my inspiration to fly.

—Mom

CONTENTS

INTRODUCTION

BUTTERFLIES AND BOARDROOMS

I often compare my life to that of a butterfly. They start out in the world as a small and vulnerable creature that can only get so far in life in the form that it is born in. It crawls around exploring the limits that life has placed in front of it. Then one day, a very necessary transformation must occur in order to become what it was created to be. It goes into this solitary place known as a chrysalis where it is isolated from the rest of the world for a set period of time. This process must occur to evolve and transform. While it is in this solitary place, it is transforming into something different but beautiful.

When the transformation is complete, the butterfly must make its way out of the chrysalis. Movement starts the process of breaking free. If it gets help emerging, the wings will never develop properly, and it won't be able to fly. The movement of the wings and the fight is what allows fluid to reach its wings before it can take flight. So, as it fights its way out of this chrysalis, it becomes stronger.

Finally, it emerges as a new and evolved version of itself with wings to fly. There are no more limits to where it can go and what it can do. It has achieved a great milestone because not all caterpillars make it to becoming a butterfly, just like all people may not evolve beyond who they are today.

In my own life, it was very necessary to go through transformations in order to grow. It took time and some struggles to reach my goals and dreams. Some days I thought I would never get there. Some days I thought I couldn't go on. But the fight in me wouldn't let me give up. I learned that each day I struggled was a day that I was getting closer to my own emergence and flight. Finally, I made it to a version of myself that allows me to share my experiences, failures, setbacks, disappointments, successes, and triumphs as inspiration and proof that obstacles are many times part of our life journey and process. The phases are what I call the Butterfly Code Framework. This book will explain the framework this code encompasses along with examples from my life journey that I had to crawl, evolve, transform, and emerge through.

****

When I was around twelve, our house caught on fire and caused my mother, brother, and I to move to a very different side of the town than I had lived for my whole life up until that point. For my mother, it was a much better neighborhood for us, but I hated it at first because all of my friends, much of my family, and everyone who looked like me were in our old neighborhood. So, at a young age, I had to learn to interact with people who were different from me. It wasn't what I was accustomed to, but I quickly learned to adapt.

We looked different from 99 percent of our neighbors, so I didn't go outside as much. I spent a lot of alone time in my bedroom dreaming. I didn't know exactly what I wanted to be when I grew up, but watching my mother get dressed up for work as a teenager and watching movies made me often dream of business suits and boardrooms. I dreamed of briefcases and business meetings. I dreamed of executives and power lunches. I dreamed of vacations at the beach and Disney World. I never imagined those things would actually become a part of my life at that age. What I didn't realize back then is that the circumstances in my life were setting the stage for my story. Everything in your life happens for a specific reason that you may not totally understand when it's happening. I didn't understand then that the fire in our home that caused us to move was putting me in a place to learn to have friends of all races. This would become an important part of my journey because the life that I was destined to live would sometimes put me in situations where I may be the only person of my race or gender in the room, and I would need to be comfortable with that. It also showed me that there was a world outside of the neighborhood that I had spent my entire life in, and it sparked curiosity of what else was out there. Curiosity and dreaming are what would eventually take my life to places that I would have never imagined.

Dream big for yourself, and don't let anyone or anything stop you from reaching your goals and desires. If you are in the same place and situation this year as you were last year, you aren't living; you are just existing. Just because things aren't given to you doesn't mean you can't achieve them. My story is a journey of starting out in a small, inner-city neighborhood to go on to working on some of the biggest and most innovative technology projects at one of the largest companies in the world and eventually mentoring other Dreamers to follow their dreams.

During my journey, I transformed into the version of myself that I was born to be, and my vision of the Butterfly Code came to life. As I tell my story, I will summarize with small pieces of advice that have helped me soar that I call FlutterBytz. A byte in technology is a small piece of information. I hope these small pieces of information will help guide you into transformation and emerging the way it has for me.

The Butterfly Code:

- Preparation: You must crawl before you can fly.
- Evolve: You aren't meant to stay a caterpillar.
- Transformation: Embrace change while being still in your chrysalis.
- Emerge: Strengthen your wings.
- Transcend and Soar: This is where you are meant to be!

STEP ONE

PREPARATION:

YOU MUST CRAWL
BEFORE YOU CAN FLY

CHAPTER 1

DREAMING BIG ON THE GROUND

I was eighteen years into my career as a Black woman in technology before I realized that being in that position meant something special. I had become accustomed to being one of the only, if not the only, woman on a technology team. I had become accustomed to looking around and not seeing any other Black people besides myself in the room. It was a very normal part of my life and my career. I was for sure the only Black woman and sometimes Black person in many of my college classes, so I didn't expect work to be very different. I was writing computer code for a living, and many of my friends and family couldn't even wrap their minds around what that meant. Attempting to explain it was difficult if you weren't into technology. Transitioning into business analysis and project management roles eventually put me in the presence of more women, but as a software engineer, it was usually just me. In 2015, I began to really start taking diversity and inclusion (D&I) in the workplace more seriously when I learned that according to the National Center for Women & Information Technology (NCWIT) statistically, that year, only 24 percent of the

U.S. technology workforce were women, and only 3 percent were Black women.[1] Only 3 percent! That number was mind-blowing to me. How could that be? Why was that? How could we change that? Those were all of the questions that began swirling around in my head.

That was the year that my eyes opened up a bit, and I realized that I was kind of a technology unicorn. No wonder I was typically the only one in the room. That year, my life and career journey began to make sense to me. I started having a real sense of purpose. It wasn't just about coming to work every day, doing my job, and going home. A passion sparked in me that had probably been simmering for a while, but I didn't know exactly what it was. It was a feeling that had been dormant but longing to be awakened. It was something that burned inside of me that always made me feel like I was supposed to be someone different and have a purpose that was bigger than myself. I had no idea that my life was about to take me on a ride that I had to buckle up for because I was going to have to step out of my comfort zone. In a very short amount of time, young girls would begin telling me that I was an inspiration for them as a woman in technology making a difference. My story began to unfold in a way that I could look back at and know exactly why it had all happened the way that it did. Everything in my life had led up to where I was for a reason. I went from a small, limited caterpillar to transforming and emerging as a powerful butterfly, and I had no idea that the years I spent crawling was preparing me for who I was meant to be. So, let me start at the beginning.

It amazes me how the things that can bring you down can be the same things that build you up. When people get into tough situ-

1 Catherine Ashcraft, Brad McLain, and Elizabeth Eger, "Women in Tech: The Facts," National Center for Women & Information Technology, 2016, https://wpassets.ncwit.org/wp-content/uploads/2021/05/13193304/ncwit_women-in-it_2016-full-report_final-web06012016.pdf.

ations, some will wonder why it is happening to them, while others will determine what lesson they can learn from it. It took me over forty years to learn that all of the not-so-ideal situations in my life have contributed to the good within and around me. The trials and tribulations that I had to overcome have made me the person that I became. I wouldn't trade in my life for any other.

From a young age, I knew my life would be much bigger than the place that I was in. Most of my family grew up and lived on the eastern side of Pittsburgh. I have a very large, but close, family that is the foundation I was raised on. In my house as a child, there was only my mother, my older brother, and me. However, my maternal grandmother had four brothers and four sisters, which means I have a ton of aunts, uncles, and cousins who are all very significant people in my life. Within a fifteen-minute walk or drive, I could be at a family member's house, which was wonderful as a child because all of the people I loved were just a few minutes away. It created a comfort zone and a security blanket that held us all close, so leaving that comfort zone wasn't normal. I love my family wholeheartedly, but by my senior year in high school, I started wondering what was out there beyond the eastern side of Pittsburgh.

1993 wasn't a good year in the inner city. Kids my age were impacted by growing violence between rival neighborhoods. After the snow melted from the blizzard of 1993, the body of a guy many of my friends knew was found in the woods, and many young guys were going to jail for various reasons. It became a very depressing situation that I wanted to get away from. I had already known that going to college was a must, but I soon realized that college was going to be my only way out.

After graduating high school, I wanted to attend Morgan State University in Baltimore, Maryland. I got accepted, went to orientation, took all of my placement exams, and picked all of my classes. I was later disappointed by learning that I couldn't afford to attend. It was an out-of-state school, so the tuition was higher, and there were no grants or scholarships being offered to me. As disappointing as that was, I was also accepted into the University of Pittsburgh and was given a partial scholarship. Pitt is a great school, but going there meant that I had to remain in Pittsburgh for at least another four years, and I wouldn't get to experience going away to college because it was only fifteen minutes from my home. I didn't understand the lesson then, but I now know that when one door closes, it's because the one that you are destined to walk through is being opened. So, I enrolled in the University of Pittsburgh, and that part of my journey began.

I remember the first time I watched the movie *Boomerang* with Eddie Murphy and Halle Berry and envisioned myself going to work for some big corporation in a tall building with a business suit and stylish haircut. While we should all strive to be unique individuals, visualization is an important aspect in dreaming of your goals by seeing something you want to achieve. Even though my mother wasn't in corporate America, I watched her get dressed in a nice business suit every day and go to work, so that was my image of success. I knew corporate America was the place I wanted to be.

After many years of going to school in the evening, my mother earned a business degree and often had titles like executive director of something in the nonprofit world, so naturally I started to follow in her footsteps. In high school, I started taking entrepreneurship classes offered at Pitt or through my mother's job where they had youth programs. I took a course called Business Computer Applications. This class was mainly learning word processing, presentations, and spreadsheets. It was self-paced, but I eventually got to a portion of the curriculum that the teacher had never needed to teach before. It had advanced functions within spreadsheets like creating charts and graphs out of data.

At this point, I didn't have a love for technology per se but for figuring things out. I enjoyed logic and critical thinking. So, I had to figure out this portion of the class on my own, and when I did, I began helping and teaching it to other class members. I loved it so much that I went to talk to my guidance counselor about being intrigued by computers.

It made me remember playing around with a Commodore 64 when I was about ten or eleven. It had this book where you had to type in all this stuff that didn't make any sense to me, but if you did it right, it would play a specific sound or do something special. You had to type it in exactly right, and if you didn't, you had to spend hours trying to figure out what was wrong. Something was out of place or misspelled, and I had to find it. The reward was finally getting it to work. I didn't know at the time that was my first taste of computer programming. That stuff in that book was lines of code for specific commands or functions. So, my guidance counselor talked to me about computer science, and I was hungry to learn more.

During my very last semester of my senior year, he recommended that I take a computer programming course called Turbo Pascal. I did, but when I walked into the class, I noticed something right away. Not only was I the only Black person, which was not unusual to me, but I was also the only girl. That was new to me! It was a small class of maybe eight all-male students who probably didn't sit with what would be considered the cool kids in the lunch cafeteria.

At the time, I was the captain of our cheerleading team and pretty popular. But now there I was sitting in a classroom of people who didn't appear to be anything like me. I think back to this because I could have easily gone to get a class change because I didn't have any friends in this class or anyone that I would even become friends with. It definitely made me feel like it wasn't a class girls would normally take. I didn't like that at all, but I wanted to explore it, and so I stuck it out. It turned out that the class wasn't easy. For the first time, a class wasn't easy for me, and that made me like it even more. What I also learned is that, even though the people in the class didn't look like me, we did have something in common: a desire to learn more about technology, and despite not looking like I belonged in the class, I was a tech nerd just like them.

When my guidance counselor checked in on me and found out how much I really liked it, he gave me some information about a research program at Carnegie Mellon University. A program that would pay me $100! I went to a small computer lab where they gave me very little instructions and sat me at a computer. I had to make my way through a series of problems. Problems that were patterns and I had to figure out what the next pattern would be. I was using a computer language called Prolog and Lisp, which I learned only recently that I had been introduced to artificial intelligence back then. I had no idea what those symbols meant or what I was doing, but I worked my way through a series of patterns until I earned my $100. That was the moment that I knew I wanted a career doing something in computer programming.

My very first technology job in college was because a friend of mine, who was a computer science major, offered me a job in the computer lab on campus. I soon found a true love for technology and became really good at helping people with problems in the computer lab. I eventually chose information science as my major instead of computer science. This major was kind of new, but it was more of a mix of business and technology. I had to take classes like Public Speaking, Economics, and Business Professional Writing, along with Systems Analysis, Object-Oriented Programming, Statistics, and Symbolic Logic. It was the perfect mix of the things that I loved, and I was so excited to tell my mother that I had decided on a major. I had researched job openings in the school paper to see what the potential salary could be, and my mind was made up.

The reaction I got was totally not what I expected. I was shocked that my mother was unsupportive of that decision. She wanted me to major in business because that's what she knew and understood. I will never forget her telling me that I wasn't going to like working with computers and that I would be pigeonholed if I chose this route. As much as I tried to explain that I was passionate about working in technology and that this was the way the world was going now, she wouldn't accept it. The next exchange of words would forever be ingrained in my memory. I showed her the newspaper of the starting salary right out of college, and her words stabbed me straight in the heart. I can still hear the words in my mind: "But you won't make that kind of money because you are Black." The look on my face must have shown the disbelief, shock, and horror that was going on in my mind because she responded by saying, "I'm just telling you this because it's the truth."

I left that conversation feeling disappointed, heartbroken, and kind of angry. But before anyone paints the picture of my mother being a terrible person, I know my mother said these things because that was what she knew and had experienced in her life and that was what she truly believed. She grew up in an era where racism was blatant and directly in your face. At that time, we didn't have many people in my family who were making six-figure salaries, so for me to say that I one day aspired to have that was a dream. Technology careers were something she was unfamiliar with and didn't understand, so she was trying to protect me from failure and disappointment. She was trying to keep me safe from all the ugliness in this world without knowing that she was shattering my dreams. That conversation didn't stop me. I used it as fuel to the fire that burned inside of me to do great things in life. From that day on, I was on a mission to show her something different.

Even though I would eventually prove that I would be successful, she was right that being Black would introduce me to the concept of the gender and racial pay gap. So even though I did eventually get a great job making great money, it would be different from what some of my peers made. I later learned to appreciate what she said to me. She wasn't telling me I wouldn't be successful but was preparing me for what I may face being Black in corporate America.

FlutterBytz:

• Don't let anyone kill your dreams! Everyone doesn't have the same vantage point as you do, and that's OK. Let's compare a caterpillar to a butterfly. There is nothing wrong with being a caterpillar, but do not be upset if you're a butterfly and the caterpillars can't even begin to imagine what it's like to fly. They're only familiar with what's on the ground because they haven't transformed into a butterfly yet. Everyone isn't made the same, and everyone isn't made to have the same types of goals and dreams. Some dreams are small and that's OK. Some dreams are bigger than people can even imagine and that's OK, too. Just keep striving toward your goals.

• Parents, please do not kill or shatter your children's dreams just because you don't understand them. We often want our children to follow in our footsteps, but we should want them to go on and do greater things. Sit down and have them help you understand what their dreams, desires, and goals are and then encourage them to go after them. While they are young, their dreams may change one hundred times. But, when they find their true passion, encourage and support them because they will need it.

CHAPTER 2

A WHOLE NEW WORLD

I was close to finishing my junior year in college knowing without a doubt technology was the career that I wanted to pursue. I was walking through the student union one afternoon when, out of the corner of my eye, I saw Mickey Mouse on a sign. I stopped what I was doing and went over to read the poster that was on the wall. It was an advertisement about a college program at Disney World, and they were having an information session later that evening. I was so excited that I called one of my cousins who was also attending Pitt and said, "Let's go to Disney World!"

We attended the information session and signed up for an interview the next day. A few weeks later, we were both accepted, and that fall we would be spending a semester working at the happiest place on Earth. I was ecstatic! I knew that having the opportunity to put Disney on my résumé and to learn the operations of one of the best companies in the world was going to open up many doors for me.

Needless to say, my cousin and I boarded a plane that August of 1996 and embarked on a journey to a whole new world. From the moment I arrived in Orlando, I knew my life would never be the same. It was the first time moving away from home, the first time truly being on my own, my first taste of true independence, and the first time that I would leave home not knowing what to expect but not afraid to try. I moved into student housing, and my job for the next four months would be as a greeter at what was then called MGM Studios. I had only been to Disney World once when I was twelve years old, so everything felt pretty new to me. This particular park didn't exist when I had visited, and it ended up being my favorite.

Even though my career goals were to work in technology, I didn't mind one bit that I would be working at the turnstiles at the front of the park checking people's tickets. I was sometimes the first smiling face that people saw when they arrived at the park or the last smiling face they saw when they left. Each day I got to watch the Toy Story parade make its way down Hollywood Boulevard. I probably ended up on several people's video cameras dancing with their children. I learned that this place was magical, and it made both children and adults feel like the happiest people in the world. The excitement that people got in the presence of Mickey Mouse was something you couldn't get anywhere else, and I felt proud to be a part of such an amazing company. But most of all, I felt extreme inspiration by learning about Walt Disney, his values, and the company mission, which is something I would carry with me for the rest of my life.

Walt Disney is one of the biggest examples of dreaming big that I began to follow from the time I was twenty-one years old and working in that program. Learning about his life was such an inspiration. I didn't know that he had other companies that he failed at and had to declare bankruptcy. I didn't know that he had lost the rights to one of his first successful animated characters, Oswald the

Lucky Rabbit. Can you imagine having a successful company with something that you created that's doing extremely well, but you lose it? In my eyes, that was a huge setback or maybe even what some would consider a failure. But Walt Disney kept moving forward and created Mickey Mouse, a character that would later turn the company into what it is today because he never gave up and always dreamed big.

After the program, I returned to Pittsburgh in January to complete my last year of college. I didn't view Disney as a technology company, so I didn't consider trying to stay or pursuing a career any further. I was supposed to graduate that December; however, that summer, I started an internship with U.S. Steel. I was required to commit to an entire year for the internship. So instead of taking summer classes, I moved those classes to the spring so that I would graduate in April. Why was this important? It's almost impossible to get a good technology job right out of college without experience. I worked full-time over the summer, where I was trained in Cobol, JCL, and Db2. Then I worked twenty hours a week during the fall and spring while I took classes either in the evenings or on days when I didn't work. This turned out to be a great decision.

That fall, I started going to campus job fairs and trying to establish my life after college. I knew I wanted to leave Pittsburgh, and I had my sight set on Maryland. It was close enough to Pittsburgh to be able to drive back whenever I needed to but far enough to say I no longer lived in Pittsburgh. I put on a gray business suit that my mother had given me as I started my interviewing journey. I had about thirty copies of my résumé in my nice University of Pittsburgh portfolio, and I was ready. I walked around the job fair and looked for big-name companies that I knew were in Maryland. I gathered all of the information that I needed from everyone, signed up for campus interviews for the next day, and was heading out the door. Right before I reached it, a man approached me from a booth that was close to the exit and asked me if I ever considered a career with IBM. I knew IBM was a huge company, but, for some reason, I thought they weren't around anymore. When I thought about big-name technology companies, Microsoft was always the first company that came to mind.

Later that evening, I took a seat among many of my classmates at an information session about the company. Everything was going great until they said they were looking to recruit people for their offices in New York and New Jersey. Since I didn't want to live in either of those cities, I began heading for the door. Once again, right before I got there, something stopped me. I heard the man mention that they would be doing on-campus interviews the next morning for positions in Atlanta, Georgia. I had never thought about moving to Atlanta because it was so far away, but I always heard it was a great place to live. So I sat back down and stayed for the rest of the session, mainly because the name of the interviewer mentioned was the boyfriend of a very good friend of mine. If he was in town doing interviews, I knew exactly where I could find him that evening. He had graduated the year before, and I had heard that he was working at IBM in Atlanta, but I never gave it any thought.

I left the information session and headed straight to my friend's house, and sure enough he was sitting there on her couch. I didn't know her boyfriend very well, but I knew him enough to talk to him about IBM and Atlanta. I showed him my résumé and studied his face as he glanced over it. He told me that out of all of the résumés he had seen over the past few days, mine probably had the best skills for what they were looking for. It was 1997, and the whole Year 2000 or Y2K debacle was a hot topic. What that means is that older computer systems only allowed you to put in two digits for the year. "19" was hard coded, and so you would be required to enter "97" to make up the year 1997. Well, when the year 2000 came around in a few years, if you enter "00," the computer system would think it was 1900 and completely get all out of whack. It would become a complete nightmare especially for banking systems. Most of these older systems were written in Cobol, and there weren't many programmers who knew it because it was an older programming language. So, my internship was a blessing in disguise, or as I later learned, a part of my journey. He took my résumé back to Atlanta and said he would put it in the pile of résumés that he recommended for an in-person interview. I left that evening feeling like I already had this job. It was like God planted it into my heart, and I was just following the lead. The way things had fallen into place that day was strange, and it seemed to me that my steps were ordered by placing me in the right place at the right time.

About a week later, I had come home from class and was getting ready to start my homework when I got a call from a recruiter at IBM asking if I would be interested in flying to Atlanta for an interview. Of course, I said yes! I was given the details that I would fly down on a Thursday for an information session and dinner at the Renaissance Hotel by the Atlanta airport. I would stay at the Renaissance for one night. During my stay, I would have breakfast Friday morning, two morning interviews, lunch, and then two more interviews in the afternoon. I would fly back out immediately following the interview and be back home in Pittsburgh by Friday night. The company was paying for everything. All I had to do was follow the instructions and get on the plane.

Two weeks later, I was heading to Atlanta. I had never been on a plane alone before, so I was very nervous about the entire trip. Flying by myself, being in Atlanta by myself, and going on my first major interview with a Fortune 500 company were all things to be nervous about. Back then, I didn't have a cell phone or a smartphone to help me. All directions were mailed on paper—not even emailed. But I knew I would be able to handle it.

I vividly remember walking through the Atlanta airport and how busy it was. It was nothing like the Pittsburgh airport. I grabbed my garment bag from baggage claim and headed to ground transportation as I was instructed. I looked for the Renaissance shuttle van, got on, and took a seat. I could see the hotel directly on the other side of the runway all lit up because it was nighttime at this point. By the time I had the chance to gather my thoughts and think about being in Atlanta, it was time for me to get off the shuttle and check in. I walked into the hotel and was completely blown away. I looked up at the hundreds of rooms that overlooked the lobby. The marble floors and the soft sound of a piano put me in a relaxed mood. I went over to the desk, checked in, and got my key. The elevator was completely glass, and I could still see the beauty of the lobby as I ascended to the eighth floor. When I opened the door to my room, I laughed to myself as I dropped my bag on the floor and ran into the most luxurious room I had ever been in. I dove on the plush, king-sized bed and thanked God for just granting me the opportunity to be there. I walked into the bathroom and couldn't believe that there were miniature bottles of toiletries from Bath & Body Works sitting on the counter. Even though I didn't know if I would get this job or not, I felt like I had made it. Never in a million years had I imagined that any company would be flying me, a girl from a single-parent family in the inner city, to a place like this and paying for it all. I jumped on the bed, closed my eyes, and just savored the moment.

The plane ride back was calmer than the ride down. I wasn't nervous anymore because I felt great about how the day went. I looked out the window and watched the city of Atlanta become small and soon disappear. I smiled to myself because I knew Atlanta had not seen the last of me. I went through four interviews earlier that day. By the time I made it to my third interview, I knew I had a future with IBM. Everyone kept asking me the same questions, which was how I had gotten the specific computer skills that I had and what it was like working at Disney. It wasn't the classroom experience that they were impressed with but the real-world programming experience that I had gained at my internship at U.S. Steel. I had picked up a skill that was no longer taught in the classroom, but it was something that every technical company needed right during that time. Knowing Cobol, Db2, IMS, and JCL really was a blessing because of the Y2K issue. I look back at that and know it was no mistake that I was selected for that internship. I made the right decision in extending my year out, and that step was necessary for this part of my journey. So, when I got to the last interview, the manager told me that he had already been hearing great things about me and that if I didn't get an offer from the company, I should give him a call. I stored his business card away in a safe place. I never wanted to live in Atlanta, but the way things had worked out, I felt like there was a plan for me there. Everything had fallen into place so easily that I felt it couldn't be anything other than what was destined for me.

A week later, I had just completed my statistics final, and I was feeling good about it. I felt good about my grades as I was finishing up my next to last semester before earning my bachelor's degree. I commuted to school my last year because, after I returned from Disney, I just wasn't interested in living on campus. So, when I arrived home, there was an Airborne Express package sitting on the table. I saw that it was from IBM. I immediately got excited because it was a thick package. A rejection letter is only one page and can easily fit in an envelope, so I knew this couldn't be a rejection. I tore open the package and began reading the letter.

"WE ARE PLEASED TO OFFER YOU A POSITION WITH IBM'S GLOBAL SERVICES AS AN INFORMATION TECHNOLOGY SPECIALIST WITH AN ANNUAL SALARY OF $45,000. WE WILL SUPPLY YOU WITH $5,000 TO RELOCATE TO ATLANTA, GA."

I didn't read any further; I just started screaming. I couldn't believe it. U.S. Steel had also offered me a full-time position that was $10,000 less than IBM, but every part of me was ready to get away and be on my own. I couldn't really figure out what it was I was trying to get away from, but I knew it was time to spread my wings and fly out of Pittsburgh. IBM had just provided me with my one-way ticket. There was something in me that was pulling me toward something else that I wouldn't find in Pittsburgh. I accepted the offer. That spring, I would be embarking on the next big journey of my life.

****

Atlanta is where I thought I would live happily ever after, but in the end, my journey there was a whirlwind. It was 1998 when I arrived. I was twenty-three years old and was completely on my own for the first time. I didn't know one single person in Atlanta other than my friend's boyfriend, but I didn't care. It was time for me to start my new life. IBM would open up my world to travel, training, business meals, and everything I thought a technology career would be. Four months after moving there, I would meet the person who would become my husband. I bought my dream house two years later at twenty-five years old. It had four bedrooms, 2,700 square feet, and everything I needed in a home.

However, the same year that I bought my home we were both laid off from IBM. I had done everything that I thought I was supposed to do in life up until that point. I graduated from college, got a great job, and bought a big house. Then I lost the job. I had to quickly learn that life isn't always what you expected it to be. I was ashamed and embarrassed and didn't really tell anybody that we had both lost our jobs. Going back home would have been a failure to me. I had to figure it out and keep moving forward.

Luckily we had severance packages, so we were able to live for about a year without a job until I eventually found a new position at another technology company. The lesson that I learned is that no company is loyal to you. So from there on, I decided to only spend about two to three years at one company before I would move on to something new.

We were able to get back on our feet and try to continue our happily ever after. In 2004, I became a mother, and my entire life changed. It was the best feeling in the world, and I was super excited to have a daughter. I was hoping to get back on track to my happily ever after, but I started going through the most painful time of my life. By the time she was four, I would be going through a separation and then a divorce.

FlutterBytz:

- Trust the process! Sometimes we may have a plan or path in our minds of what we may want to do and get disappointed when it doesn't turn out the way we have planned. However, if we stop and allow the path to unfold, it may turn out to be a bigger dream than we ever imagined for ourselves.
- In some cases, the path on your journey may take you down a path that you didn't expect. The adversity, struggles, and pain may also be a part of your journey and process to force you to start changing into a more evolved version of yourself.

STEP TWO

EVOLVE:

YOU AREN'T MEANT TO
STAY A CATERPILLAR

CHAPTER 3

ADULTING, DISAPPOINTMENTS, AND DEPRESSION

Soon after my daughter was born, I was miserable in my marriage but refused to admit it to myself or anyone else. I was feeling like an eagle trapped in a cage. I knew that my life was meant to be something more than it had become, and I knew that I couldn't get to where I was going in the situation that I was in. I pondered and thought about it for years. I tried to make things work for the sake of my daughter being in a complete family, but after ten years together, I had finally found the strength to leave the marriage.

I didn't understand it at the time, but my marriage was emotionally and mentally abusive. It wasn't the best place for myself or my daughter, and, as painful as it was, I had to make the decision to leave it. So, in 2009, I began going through a very stressful divorce, and, for the next two years, I began to have emotional, mental, and financial struggles. My two-income household was now a one-income household, and I became something that I hoped I would never have to be: a single mother. My ex-husband moved out of the state and eventually took a job overseas. I had no family in Atlanta, so my first instinct was to pack up everything and move back to Pittsburgh so that I could have the security blanket of my family.

During this time, I started a journey of inner healing and getting more in touch with my spiritual self. This was a life-changing experience for me because during those two years, I would go through various ups, downs, and periods of depression. Like most mothers, my child is what kept me going each day. My life was no longer just about me. There was someone depending on me and looking up to me, so I had to pray multiple times daily just to make it through the next few hours. I would drop my four-year-old daughter off at school in the morning, cry during my one-hour commute to work, wipe my tears, pull myself together, walk into work with my head held high, work all day, get into my car, fall apart and cry during my one-hour commute back, pull into the parking lot of my daughter's school, wipe my tears, pull it together again, and have a smile on my face when I picked her up. I made it a point to never let her see that anything was wrong.

Since I had started a spiritual journey during that time, I understood clearly that this was a part of my story and journey that was always in the plans for me. It helped me understand that growing up without a father in my home and being raised by a single mother prepared me for what I was going through. My mother had made it through with two children and half the income, so I knew that I would be able to make it. I empathize with how my daughter felt about her father no longer being around, so I knew exactly what to say and what not to say to her to help her get through it.

I began to have a lot of clarity. Instead of becoming a victim and crying over the why, I began to pray for the how. How could I use this time of disappointment as a lesson or a way to become stronger and move forward with my life? I didn't pray for another husband or a new man in my life, because after coming out of a ten-year relationship, I needed to get to know myself. I needed to focus on who I wanted to be and how I could be the best mother possible. I wanted to give my child my undivided attention because we both needed each other to make it. She needed me as her mother, and I needed her as my inspiration. She was my motivation to keep moving forward—to be the best role model I could be for her and to set an example and standard of the type of woman she would one day want to grow up to be. I wanted to be the type of mother and woman whom my daughter was going to be proud of. So, I started working on myself personally, and I prayed constantly. It was time to evolve from being a caterpillar, and I knew the evolution was going to take me out of my comfort zone once again.

****

I want to point out something important. It took two years of prayers with no answers. It took two years of just sitting still and being quiet. I had to make sacrifices in my career so that I could make being a mother my first priority. I put climbing the corporate ladder on hold because working late and putting in extra hours at night was not an option for me. It didn't mean that I faced a setback—it just meant that I couldn't move forward for a couple of years. I had to start the process of going into my chrysalis and allow my transformation to take place. So, please note, the answers you seek may not come right away and may take longer than you anticipate. But, understand that there is something bigger that may need to happen that doesn't always include you directly. Patience is very important. While I was waiting for answers, I learned that there were things happening in my favor that I had to allow to unfold even though I didn't understand it at the time.

****

Every New Year, I set goals for myself. I always felt like if I wasn't working toward something, I wasn't advancing in my life. But sometimes, we just have to take a break and sit still. I prided myself on always being in control of my life and being able to handle every obstacle that got in my way. But sometimes, whatever your spiritual guidance is will knock you all the way down just to get your attention. You may be put in a place where you feel like no one is there for you just so that you can totally depend on your guiding force. I was so tired of trying to find the strength to stand that when the New Year of 2011 came around, I didn't set a goal. I was so afraid that I was going to make more mistakes in my life that I didn't want to make any more decisions without knowing that it was what my God wanted for me.

This time of sitting still was my time of connecting with my spirituality more deeply. Sometimes we have to get quiet and just listen. We need to be able to know the difference between our own voice, our God's voice, and the voice of outside influences that may steer us down the wrong path. So, that New Year, I prayed to reveal what was destined for me. I was so emotionally and mentally beat down that I asked to just be carried for a while. I gave up the wheel, got into the back seat of my life, and just went along for the ride. What I learned is that what's meant for us is way bigger than what we could ever imagine or want for ourselves if we just trust and believe. So, I just sat still and waited. During that waiting period, a place was being prepared just for me, and when it was time, it was presented.

During my one-hour commute each morning to work, I would listen to *The Steve Harvey Morning Show*. I listened when he first talked about the Disney Dreamers Academy, which was a program where Walt Disney World brings one hundred high school students to the resort for a four-day, immersive experience on "dreaming big." I remember thinking to myself how amazing that would be for kids and how I wished I could have been a part of something like that when I was in high school. It made me remember the amazing experiences I had working at Disney when I was in college. So, I looked it up online and spoke out loud, "I would love to be a part of something like that one day."

I listened when Steve was broadcasting live from a Disney cruise ship, and I told myself that one day, I was going to take my daughter on a Disney Cruise. In the fall of 2010, we took our first Disney Cruise while I was still waiting on direction. While I loved everything about Disney, that cruise was the best time of my life. I had taken my daughter to Disney World twice, we had been to Las Vegas to see *The Lion King* on stage, we had been to New York to see *The Little Mermaid* on Broadway, but nothing compared to being out in the middle of the ocean with the magic of Disney all around us. I told myself that God willing, we would take a Disney Cruise each year as our vacation. Since I was working at Delta Airlines at the time, I had the ability to fly anywhere in the world for free, and every time we took a trip, it was something related to Disney.

It made me think about the lyrics of the song, "A dream is a wish your heart makes when you're fast asleep." I wasn't praying about a new job or career, I wasn't praying about moving to a new city, but when I spoke things out loud about what I wanted, I watched some of the most amazing things manifest in ways I would have never imagined. So, the day that I got a call from a recruiter at a big company in Orlando asking if I was interested in a business analyst position, I didn't hesitate to say yes.

I had applied for a few jobs in the Orlando area after our cruise in October 2010 since I had lived there before. I saw a few positions, posted my résumé, and never thought anything else about it. I wasn't seriously considering it at the time—I just put a résumé out there just to see what would happen. That curiosity planted a seed. Being willing to try something just to see what happens put my résumé into a candidate database, so when they started recruiting for this particular project, my résumé came up as a match. I hadn't applied for this particular position, but this is when I knew that the universe was working things out on my behalf. From the moment I got the first call, I said to myself, "I'm about to move to Florida!" Just moments before I got the call, moving to Florida was the farthest thing from my mind, but I knew that I had been praying for direction, and I knew this was the direction that I was waiting for.

****

Because I was growing spiritually, a few weeks prior, I started really cleaning out unnecessary stuff from my house. I had just had one of those days when I was feeling particularly down because I wasn't getting the answers I needed. I was on my knees in my family room crying and praying for answers. I remembered looking out the windows and seeing the large trees in my backyard swaying back and forth. It must have been the winds of change blowing because the next day, I decided to start cleaning out my clutter. I had ten years of stuff that had accumulated, and I kept hearing this voice and having this feeling in my spirit that said, "Get ready." (Preparation!) It was like something was telling me that change was coming. That was the day that I got the call about this new opportunity.

Everything quickly fell into place. I did the phone interview with the hiring manager and was asked to fly down for an in-person interview a few days later. It was the last week of May 2011 and also my daughter's last week of school. Just as I was trying to figure out what to do with her while I flew to Florida for the interview, my ex-husband, who I hadn't heard from in a few months, called to let me know he was in the States to surprise his oldest son who was graduating high school. When I say that the universe was working things out in my favor, believe it. He picked her up, and I made my way to Orlando.

When something is meant to be, you will have this feeling within your spirit of overpowering joy. From the moment I landed in Florida, I knew that this was going to be home again. I checked into my hotel that happened to be right by what was still called Downtown Disney, and, even though I hadn't lived there since 1996, it felt like home again. I said a prayer of thanks and to prepare me for whatever was to come. It wasn't a matter of if I got the job but when I would start the job. I put it into my mind that this position was mine and pulled out my computer to start looking at the cost of living and houses for rent. I looked at school ratings and childcare centers in the area. I was doing all of these before I even made it to the interview. (More preparation!) By the time I landed back in Atlanta that Friday, I knew in my heart that I would soon be saying goodbye to Atlanta, Georgia. This chapter of my story was coming to a close, and I was ready to evolve.

The next Tuesday, I got a call from the recruiter offering me the job. He asked me about my salary requirements, and I asked for $10,000 more than what I was currently making. He told me he could offer that as well as a relocation package that would be sent to me to review. (We are often afraid to ask for what we want because we think we aren't worth it. Just ask! The only thing we can be told is "no.") I accepted and waited for my official offer package to come in the mail. Everything was working out so perfectly that I knew this had to be the answer to my prayers. Everything was going to be taken care of with my relocation, including the sale of my house in Atlanta. All I had to do was get on a plane with my daughter and go. The movers would pack up everything and deliver it to Orlando, a real estate agent would get the house listed for sale, and I would live in temporary housing until I found somewhere permanent to live.

If I needed any more confirmation, it came right away. Soon after I was told all of the details of my relocation, I got a call back to say that there was a huge mistake. I was sent the wrong relocation package. My package was for management, and I wasn't offered a management position. However, they had to honor the package because it was already sent to me in writing and I had agreed to the terms of the package. It may have been a mistake by the company, but it was certainly no mistake to me. It was the confirmation that everything was being worked out in my favor and things were happening to show me that there were bigger plans for me. What are the odds that a large and well-known corporation would make such a mistake? I would say slim to none, but nonetheless, it was a mistake made in my favor.

Thirty days later, I sat in my empty home and looked around for the very last time. We were starting over fresh in a new city and leaving this chapter of my life behind. Before I accepted the offer, I asked my seven-year-old child if she was OK with this move. She had just finished the first grade and had a few friends whom she had been close with since she was two years old in day care. Still, she quickly told me that she would make new friends because we were moving close to Disney World and that she wanted to sit in the backyard and drink mango and papaya smoothies in Florida! As much as I knew the opportunity was the best thing for us, I didn't want to make any more major changes in her life after going through a divorce. We were stepping out completely on faith.

Stepping out on faith meant that I was leaving my home in Atlanta behind in hopes that it would sell in a terrible housing market. Stepping out on faith meant that I was about to move to a city with no friends or family as a single mother with a seven-year-old child. Stepping out on faith meant that I would find somewhere safe to live in a good school district and affordable childcare for my child. Stepping out on faith meant that I was giving up my free flight benefits with Delta Airlines, where I was working at the time, which meant I no longer had access to free flights to travel to Pittsburgh if needed or fly my mother and stepfather to me. Stepping out on faith meant that I was going to work for a new company without really knowing what to expect, but I knew that I would get a paycheck every week and I had my child and God's protection with me, which was all that I felt was needed. My daughter called it our new adventure, and that's exactly what it was. We got on a plane and embarked on that adventure.

****

The next year and a half truly was an adventure. For the first thirty days in Orlando, we lived in an extended stay hotel room until I found a place to rent. Most of our personal belongings were in storage, but we never complained. I left a four-bedroom, two-and-a-half-bathroom, 2,700-square-foot house to live in one room for thirty days. It was humbling, but it was part of the process and the journey. From that hotel room, we moved into a two-bedroom, two-and-a-half-bathroom townhouse. It was small, and I certainly didn't love it, but I kept in mind that it was a temporary living arrangement. By November, I had accepted an offer to sell my home. Selling my home was the last puzzle piece of the move, and it meant that I was not going back to Atlanta. The sale on the house closed right after Christmas, and I got my first pay raise after only being with the company for six months.

Let me take a moment to talk about my new position. I had been blessed with my dream job without knowing what my dream job really was. The company I went to was launching a top secret innovative technology project. It was one of the biggest technology projects that I had ever worked on in my entire career. I felt like I was back on track to my happily ever after, even if that happily ever after didn't include a husband and family. My happily ever after became a great career, being an amazing mother, and finding peace.

FlutterBytz:

- Evolving may be uncomfortable. It may mean stepping into the unknown. It's important to be prepared first so that when you make the decision to evolve, you've prepared yourself for your alone time.
- Evolving is a decision. Not every caterpillar will make it to become a butterfly. It has to do the things that are needed to prepare to go into its chrysalis. If it doesn't, not only will it not make it to the chrysalis, but it may not survive the chrysalis phase, as well. For me, I had to wait and prepare. When my answers came, I had to choose to evolve and leave everything I knew behind and walk toward my destiny.

STEP THREE

TRANSFORMATION:

EMBRACE CHANGE
WHILE BEING STILL IN
YOUR CHRYSALIS

CHAPTER 4

SITTING STILL AND WAITING WHILE GROWING

The chrysalis is the pupa stage of a butterfly. It's the stage where there is very little movement. Within the chrysalis is where growth and change occur. Between 2013 and 2015, I was transforming inside of my own chrysalis. There could be a lot of emotional and mental pain as well as loneliness during this stage. But I had an awareness that I was in this stage and that I was being prepared for something more.

Looking back, I realized it was a resting period. I had been through a lot up until that point, and I needed to just take a break and rest because life was about to take me places I had never imagined. From 2011 to 2013, I was in a complete transition. I had ended my career at Delta Airlines, packed up the house I had lived in for ten years and sold it, left Atlanta after living there for thirteen years, moved to Orlando to start a new life, started a new career at a new company, built and bought a new house, and helped launch one of the biggest technology projects of my career.

Things had finally stabilized. I was settled into my new home, and work had fallen into a normal day-to-day routine. I was enjoying and loving life, but then I began to question what was next. I started wondering if this was it. Was my destiny to move to Florida, be blessed with a new home and a dream job, and enjoy the rest of my life? I was content with my life. I had obtained my dream of making six figures. I was comfortable, so my next steps weren't about money or things. It was about finding a sense of purpose that had to be more than just going to work each day and coming home and being a mother. Who was I beyond that? Not that it wasn't important, but contentment has never been something I settled for.

One day I saw a post on social media that said, "God didn't bring me this far, just to bring me this far." I started praying about what was next for me. While I waited for that answer, I continued to enjoy life and work on personal and professional goals. However, I was once again reminded that what was planned for me was so much bigger than what I could ever imagine for myself, because life was about to take off very fast and unexpectedly.

****

In the later part of 2015, our technology team had formed a D&I team, which my manager asked me if I wanted to be a part of. I remember laughing and saying, "Sure, why not?" I laughed because I was the only Black person on the team, and, at that time, I felt like the word "diversity" automatically included minorities. So, naturally, I was the person they asked to be on the team. I can't remember exactly what all the goals of the team were, but there were two things that grabbed me at the very first meeting. We were shown some figures according to the National Center for Women & Information Technology. In 2015, only 24 percent of the U.S. computing workforce were women. As a woman in technology who was always one of few on a team or in a room, that number didn't shock me much.

What shocked me was that less than 10 percent of the U.S. computing workforce were women of color. Only 3 percent were African American women, 5 percent were Asian women, and 1 percent were Hispanic women.[2] Those numbers hit me in the face and stomach like bricks. It was what Oprah Winfrey calls an "aha moment." Up until that point, it was very easy for me to look at a company and say, "This company doesn't support diversity because when I look around, I'm the only person of color on the team." But to know that there truly weren't many Black women in technology could have been a big part of the reason why I don't see that many of us when I'm at work.

So, that year, it was decided that as a part of this team, we would focus on women in technology, which caused something in me to come alive. A fire lit inside of me, and things started to click. I realized that everything about my journey and my career had led me to that moment. I was a Black woman in technology who worked at a company that many people would love to work for. I was in a group that was only 3 percent of the entire U.S. workforce. I was different, and at that moment, I felt special. I felt that there was something bigger than myself that I was now going to embark upon, and I was looking forward to it. This was the start of me slowly emerging out of my chrysalis, and the events over the next few years would include some struggles that I would need to overcome in order to strengthen my wings.

****

At the very beginning of 2016, I was excited to start a new, eighteen-month-long technology project. I was more excited about

2 National Center for Women & Information Technology, "By the Numbers," accessed March 29, 2024, https://ncwit.org/resource/bythenumbers/.

this project than the last. We were expanding our technology to California, and what made me especially excited about it was that it was all brand-new work. Instead of only being responsible for one application, I started out being responsible for multiple. Since the current technology was a little older at this point, we would be creating brand-new applications. I absolutely love doing application development delivery. I love defining requirements, but I was putting my certifications and my skills in Agile development to work with this project, and it was exciting. Of course, there were many challenges and ups and downs like any technology project, but I was excited to have the opportunity to bring this project to life and grow and learn from it in the process.

Right around this same time, the movie *Hidden Figures* came out. This movie was about the lives of Katherine Johnson, Dorothy Vaughan, and Mary Jackson who were three African American women working for NASA in the 1960s. While the movie mostly centered around the life of Katherine Johnson who was a mathematician who helped put the first U.S. astronaut into space, I was most intrigued by the secondary stories of Mary Jackson, who was NASA's first Black female engineer, and Dorothy Vaughan, who taught herself the computer programming language FORTRAN. Dorothy went on to teach and prepare the Black women she supervised the language so that they could be prepared to use IBM computers.[3]

I was drawn to the strength of these women and the fact that the world didn't know that there were Black women in technology who were doing major things that they never got recognition for. There was a scene where Katherine Johnson walked into a room of all White men to start her first day on a new project, and I immediately connected to

3 *Hidden Figures*, directed by Theodore Melfi (2016; Los Angeles, CA: 20th Century Fox, 2017), DVD.

her character. Up until that point, I was often the only woman on the team, and if I wasn't, I was almost always the only Black person in the room. In 2016, I could relate to something that happened back in the '60s. I could also relate to people having no idea what I contributed to the company. I was accustomed to being in the background and playing a supporting role.

The problem was, when people asked what I did, no one could really answer. Even my leadership would just answer by saying, "She does everything." I learned that if no one knows who you are or what you do, you're not truly relevant. If you aren't relevant, your name doesn't come up when it's time for promotions. It was close to five years that I had been in the company, and I decided it was time for people to know who I was. I didn't want to remain a hidden figure. This wasn't just important for myself. I had decided that science, technology, engineering, and mathematics (STEM) outreach was a major factor in closing the gender gap in technology. We needed to start reaching young girls in middle school, high school, and college to encourage them to pursue STEM careers. In order to do that, I had to show them what a Black woman in technology working at a Fortune 500 company looked like. I had to make myself seen and heard. I had to emerge my way out of my chrysalis.

Around this time, I also created a vision board. I would write things down on sticky notes and stick them on my wall. Each morning I would wake up and read them out loud and again each night before I went to sleep. One day, I was writing out some goals, and I heard this voice say, "Inspirational speaker." I paused but ultimately ignored it. I started writing some other goals and heard the words again. I stopped and said out loud, "Are you sure about this? That's not really my thing!" I've never enjoyed being the center of attention. I've never had the desire to stand up on a stage and speak to a room full of people. But it was placed on my heart and on my mind very clearly, so I wrote it down and stuck it on the wall because something in the world had plans for me.

As a part of the technology D&I team, I was asked to also be a part of a newly created STEM Advisory Board. Both of these teams were in their infancy stage, so they were both still figuring out what these teams would look like and do. In most cases, meetings were just informational. In the STEM Advisory meetings, we'd talk about upcoming volunteer opportunities in STEM, and I would bring them back to the technology D&I team. This team provided me the opportunity to really start learning more about D&I. Diversity didn't just apply to people of color. Diversity meant anything that was different, and inclusion meant including people from many different backgrounds. So, I started thinking about how I could do things that achieved the goals of both the teams and focusing my efforts on women in STEM but, most particularly, women in technology.

Since my career in technology focuses on technology delivery, I'm a very goal-oriented person. I can't just sit around and talk about what we should do and what the problem is. Instead, I like to make a plan and take action. So, my first plan of action was to figure out how to have an impactful engagement with Disney Dreamers Academy.

I reached out to one of the coordinators and asked if I could set up some time to meet with them about an idea I had for the upcoming Disney Dreamers Academy (DDA) for 2016. I had been a volunteer for the two prior years, and although it was an amazing experience, I noticed that during the career deep dives, there wasn't a deep dive for careers in technology. Everyone included in this event was using technology to make it successful. We were missing out on the opportunity to show these students that technology powered the magic they were seeing. So, my meeting focused not just on these facts but also on

STEM and the lack of women in technology. I wanted to provide the chance to show these Dreamers how technology powers the parks they were visiting that week and also show them that there are women in technology who help make that happen. After explaining this to the DDA team, they agreed that it should be included and asked if I would put the deep dive together and facilitate it. Of course, I agreed.

What happened next was something that I will never forget. That day, the informational packages were to be sent out to the Dreamers who were accepted for that year's program. In that packet was a form where they got to select what kind of careers they were interested in. Technology wasn't even an option on the form. They were going into the ninth year of this program where technology was never an option for these Dreamers to learn about. I wondered how many opportunities we had missed to encourage someone into a technology career. So, a decision was made to redo that form and get technology added as an option. They pulled back those packages that were set to be mailed out that day so that they could be updated. It made me realize that if I had met with them just one day later, we would have missed the opportunity. I was really happy that I was able to make a difference and get that added. That alone gave me a sense of accomplishment and would start the ball rolling for many years of success facilitating the technology workshops for the program.

That year I was able to facilitate my first technology deep dive with a class of six students. What was even more amazing is that half of the class were girls! So, right away I was able to make a difference for inspiring more women in technology. What was most fulfilling was getting handwritten notes and email messages from those students telling me how much of an inspiration I was.

Later that year, I was asked to be on a panel for Women's History Month. It was the first time ever being on a panel speaking about my career as a woman in tech. Two things stood out to me. The first was that I was the only Black woman on the panel. The second was that I was the only nonexecutive on the panel. At the time I wasn't even a manager yet. So, I remembered what it felt like sitting next to what I considered women of power. Up until that point, I hadn't aspired to be a director or vice president (VP) in technology because I hadn't seen any who looked like me since I had left Atlanta. Even though the women on the panel weren't women of color, something secretly inside of me told me that I could one day be an executive. So, at that point, I had to make it known that I wanted to step into leadership and become a manager.

However, it dawned on me why I was the only Black woman on the panel who wasn't an executive. It was because there were none. When I thought about it, there were actually only a few Black managers. I immediately became discouraged because I didn't want to have to bear the burden of becoming the first. Being a woman in technology was a safe space because it was being supported by the company. Addressing the lack of Black people in technology (man or woman) wasn't so safe. If I started ringing alarm bells about it, I wasn't confident that it would be received well, supported, or cared about. So I stayed in the woman-in-tech lane and rode the wave of identifying as just that and set my sights on just being a manager.

That fall, I was invited to attend the Grace Hopper Celebration of Women in Technology Conference in Houston on behalf of the company. I was ecstatic! I was getting the opportunity to represent our company to over fifteen thousand women and even had the chance to do some tech talks in the booth. However, what I was most proud about is that I was asked to take some marketing photos and was in several social media posts about our engagement at the event. To my surprise, when we arrived at the conference, there was a huge photo of me in the booth! I definitely felt like I had made it! I was in the marketing material for one of the biggest companies in the world. As amazing as that felt, there was also a part of me that felt like I was the token Black woman being put into the forefront to show that there were in fact Black women in technology at the company, even if I was one of just a few.

After that panel, I began expressing my desire to be promoted to manager and making my case for all the reasons that I was qualified and ready. I continued to volunteer as much of my free time as I could by going into classrooms and speaking to our youth about careers in technology. Early the next year, I was nominated and selected for one of the top awards that the company had for inspiring others through my volunteer work and asked to return to Disney Dreamers Academy to facilitate another technology workshop. This story serves as a lesson to never give up on your goals and what you believe in! After a yearlong process, in May 2017, I was promoted from a senior project manager to a manager of technology. This is what I considered breaking the glass ceiling. Although I was extremely happy and proud of that accomplishment, it didn't come easy. I was a Black woman in a male-dominated field, and there aren't many of us in the field itself, let alone in management or executive positions. I had been doing the job of a manager for a while without the title or pay. I watched men get promoted or hired into manager positions on my team without even being considered. However, I stood up for myself and started fighting for what I wanted. I realized that no one was just going to give me anything. As long as I remained silent and content, nothing would have happened even though I had earned it. Many of my team members recommended me for promotion and questioned why I hadn't been promoted yet. I was finally brave enough to state the facts: "I'm a Black woman in a white male-dominated career field. The blueprint for success will always look different for me."

There were many days I almost gave up. Many days that I wanted to walk out. Many days where I felt so defeated and emotionally exhausted. But I knew that giving up and walking out meant I was giving up on every young Black girl whom I've encouraged to pursue technology careers. I'd be giving up and walking out on my daughter who was watching me stand up for myself in this space. Many days I wanted to just shatter that glass ceiling with a baseball bat out of anger. Instead, I slowly chiseled away at it each day. I was persistent in a professional way. I refused to give up until, finally, I achieved my goal.

I love my job. I love what I do. But I never said it was easy. I help people's dreams come true with technology every single day while sometimes wondering how I can make those dreams come true for myself. Life isn't always easy. Blessings don't always come when you ask for them because sometimes you are being used for a higher purpose, which is something I understood. If I'm going to help others like me overcome the struggles of being a Black woman in the corporate technology world, then I first need to go through that struggle myself. I accepted that, and in the end, it was all worth it.

FlutterBytz:

- Your life is a journey, so pay attention to the lessons you are meant to learn while you are trying to get to your destination.

STEP FOUR

EMERGE:

STRENGTHEN YOUR WINGS

CHAPTER 5

EMERGING!

The year 2020 began by celebrating my forty-fifth birthday in Las Vegas. I was feeling amazing about all that I had accomplished in my life up until that point and was celebrating all the great projects I had successfully completed in 2019 in California and Tokyo. I was just feeling good about myself and who I was becoming and was looking forward to all that 2020 had to offer.

Three months later in March, life as we knew it changed and would continue to change for most of 2020. COVID-19 was spreading in Asia and parts of Europe, and it had rapidly started to hit the United States. In a matter of days, the country shut down. It started with everyone working remotely from home if their jobs allowed, and then businesses closed their doors in an effort to stop the spread. Schools closed and went virtual for the remainder of the school year, Orlando parks closed, merchandise stores closed, cruises were shut down, international travel stopped, professional sports were suspended, and people were restricted to their homes for months. People were losing their jobs, some were being temporarily furloughed, and fear and uncertainty set in for most people. Hospitals began to fill with thousands of people critically ill with COVID-19, and hundreds were dying daily. There was so much unknown. I had never seen anything like it in my life. The world was closed! The streets were empty.

However, some suggested the Earth was healing because it needed a break. While the pandemic was a tragic event, I focused on areas of my life that resonated with that statement. I was cooking more meals at home. My daughter and I were spending more quality time together. But, most importantly, I was resting. I took the opportunity to just sit still and wait. I'm grateful that I did because I didn't know another storm was brewing that would shake up my world in a way that would never be the same.

In May, just as people had gotten used to the "new normal," the country started to slowly reopen in phases. It was Memorial Day weekend, so I decided to drive to the beach for a change of scenery. The beach calms me, so we took the risk and kept our distance and wore masks. I had no idea that I would wake up the following morning to a video all over social media and the news of another Black man being murdered by police officers, one with his knee on this man's neck.

That man, George Floyd, would forever be remembered as the breaking point that sent the country into an uproar of protests and riots. We were tired. Enough was enough. My heart broke, and I cried watching the eight minutes and forty-five seconds that this man begged for his life, cried out to his mother, and eventually lost consciousness and died with a knee still on his neck. While people were confined to their homes with nothing more to watch but this horrific event, the country erupted into people of all colors taking to the streets to protest police brutality, and a revolution started to ripple across the world. Racial tensions were high, and everyone was listening. Racists showed their true feelings all over social media, while others who were tired of it shared that information with their employers and called for their firing. Companies started public relations campaigns and decided that "Black lives mattered," while others debated that "all lives mattered."

Here's the problem with the "all lives matter" narrative. Let's say you have two children and one of them is sick. Would you tell the sick child who needs a little more attention and help during that time that both they and their sibling matter and should be treated the same? At that moment, the sick child needs a little extra attention and care. Furthermore, if you completely ignore the fact that this child needs special attention, you can't then say that they both matter, because you are neglecting the care that one of them needs. So, if you don't care about Black lives, how can you say all lives matter?

During this time, I continued to work remotely as if nothing was different. After all, we've seen this before way too many times, but we've never carried it to work. This time, however, our companies that we work for brought it to work, and things got real.

As I mentioned before, there are not many Black females in technology. So, I had gotten used to being the only Black person on many technology teams. I had been conditioned to accept something as the norm because that's just the way it had been, when in reality that was unacceptable. Up until that point, I hadn't used my voice as loudly as I should have. There was something about companies addressing what was going internally and externally on social media that was getting under my skin. There was something about companies stating that they "stand with their Black employees and the Black communities" and proclaiming that "Black lives matter" but making work go on as usual with no one really addressing it with me directly. What did standing with me really mean when, in reality, I had never felt so alone in my entire career? Up-front racism was one thing, which I thankfully hadn't experienced in my workplace, but I had to question the lack of Black representation above the manager level. That lack had given a clear indication that no one really knew how to address why the country was on fire, why Black people were so outraged, and what it felt like to show up at work feeling isolated. I wasn't OK.

Black people across the country weren't OK, and we weren't going to continue to pretend that we were. I couldn't pretend anymore. I was angry; I was hurt; I couldn't concentrate on or care about work because I didn't feel like I mattered. I questioned if the company that I was at was the place for me anymore. Was I really valued as a person? I was stuck feeling this way for about a week when I realized that I was in a new chrysalis and wasn't sure if I was prepared for it. I was engulfed with pain and outrage, and I didn't know what to do with that. At the end of the day, I had a job to do, and I needed to be able to do it. I wasn't being paid for someone to care about my feelings, but I had to take some time off to just allow myself to not be OK in this space alone. I had to find a way to turn that pain into passion and purpose. What I realized was that my entire technology journey prepared me for this. Everything in my life up until that point was me preparing, crawling, and evolving to enter into this chrysalis that I would emerge from as an entirely new person once again.

About a week later, a vice president at my company reached out to ask how I was doing and wanted to know what he could be doing more to address social injustice to the members on his team. I took this opportunity to be completely transparent and open about how I was feeling. The silence at work had become deafening, but I realized it was because the people in my workplace at the executive level and above were not Black and they couldn't relate or have perspective on what was happening and how to address it. Our chief technology officer (CTO) didn't have anyone at the table to give him perspective on the Black experience in America and how it affects the Black people in the workplace. I explained that this was exactly why D&I was so important. What was needed were true allies that were willing to use their own power to make a difference. So, when I was asked if I would be comfortable talking to our CTO to give him my perspective, I made sure that I took that opportunity to not only provide my perspective but also provide ideas, strategies, and a plan for change. It was time for me to emerge from this chrysalis of anger and pain and start strengthening my wings to prepare to take flight and embrace who I was. I wasn't just a woman in technology, but I was a Black woman in technology, and it was time to acknowledge and address what it felt like to be in this not-so-safe space. I felt it wasn't as safe because the number of women in technology around me had begun to grow, and there seemed to be more support for women in technology initiatives, but I continued to be the only Black person on teams, and I didn't have anyone I felt could relate or understand what that felt like. Years prior, I briefly shared with a few people in the company that it was better to address the lack of Black technologists at that moment than waiting until a light was shone on the problem. Well, that time had arrived, and the light was shining bright. Every company across the country was being asked to reveal their diversity numbers, and it didn't look good.

One night, I had an epiphany. All of a sudden, Black lives were at the top of every company's agenda. The lack of Black representation in big corporations was being called out, and everyone was scrambling to try to make a difference. The epiphany: We were in demand! Companies were hiring Black talent into executive and management positions like crazy, and it would have been easy for me to write my own ticket and walk out the door. Because I loved the company that I worked for, instead of leaving, I felt empowered to use this epiphany to drive change. We had the floor, and people were listening. I knew we may never get this opportunity again, so I went on a mission to use my voice to make a change.

In my career, I've always found areas of improvement as an opportunity for myself. My CTO had a blind spot, and I made it my business to help him see through my own eyes. Not only did I explain to him the problems, but I also laid out solutions and plans. I even offered myself as someone to help drive those solutions and plans because these changes wouldn't be a sprint but a marathon.

During one of our first conversations, my CTO revealed that he was a first-generation immigrant into the United States and that he hadn't ever experienced racism in the country. His view of the country was different from those who were born here and had knowledge of the deep-rooted history of racism. He asked me to simply help him understand how we went from having a Black president to a man dying on television with a knee on his neck. Before that conversation, I don't know if our CTO really knew me, but my goal was to leave that conversation with him never forgetting me. I explained how this wasn't new to us and that these types of tragedies happen more often than we'd like and this incident was a breaking point. I explained how the first time I had witnessed something like this was when I was a senior in high school when the trials for the attack on Rodney King took place. I explained what it was like to learn of the not guilty verdict and how I would see this happen countless more times. We carry these things to work day in and day out and never bring them up. I mentioned how we've been suppressing what happened to Trayvon Martin and Michael Brown. How we were still saddened about what had happened earlier that same year with Breonna Taylor and Ahmaud Arbery. I shared with him what institutional racism was. Even though I've never experienced any outright racism within our company, when you look around and see the lack of people of color being promoted to management and executive positions when we are just as experienced if not more than those who are being promoted, we have to question why. I shared that I wholeheartedly believed that if I were not a Black woman, I'd be further along in my twenty-five-year career than I was.

I am in no way saying that I believe the company as a whole is racist, because you can't put the ways some people may think on the entire company. However, let me explain how it's very possible that you can have racist people working at a company who might be adverse to change or the advancement of people of color. If some of the people at the top of leadership have been with a company for forty-plus years or were born in the 1950s or 1960s, they or the people who raised them were alive during a time when Black people weren't allowed to vote and it was legal to discriminate based on race. My mother, who was born in 1951, was alive during a time when Black people weren't allowed to vote until 1965, and up until 1968, it was OK to discriminate. I can't imagine the things she has witnessed along with my grandparents. So, of course, she would think and believe that one day, I would be facing a hard upward battle in my career. Of course, when this situation happened with George Floyd, she would tell me to just be quiet and make sure I didn't jeopardize this good job. Of course, she would be fearful that there would be repercussions or backlash for me speaking out on what I felt needed to change because in her lifetime, she experienced race riots. In her lifetime, she's experienced blatant discrimination. She was alive when Martin Luther King Jr. and Malcom X were killed. Now here she was witnessing her only daughter stand up for the lack of Black people in technology roles, when the mentality for many is that we should just be happy and grateful that we are even here in these jobs at all.

That year I felt like I had finally found my voice. The voice was always there but had been muted. I kept quiet about what I had been witnessing my entire career because honestly, there was also probably a part of me that felt like I never even thought I'd make it this far so I wanted to take what I had and be quiet. But, my voice erupted out of the pit of my stomach like a scream! Something had to be said. Someone had to speak up. Instead of approaching the situation like Black people were still being treated unfairly in the country, I approached it business-minded. We weren't looking for a handout. We weren't asking to be given promotions and put into new positions just because we were Black but because we were qualified and had the experience. We had been looked over because we didn't fit the idea of what a technology executive looked like. We didn't look like Steve Jobs or Bill Gates. However, when it comes to D&I in business, there are reasons why you have different thoughts and people involved. A board of directors has people from different companies represented so that everyone isn't thinking the same way. On a technology delivery team, in order for a project to be successful, you need people with different skill sets to bring the project together. At a minimum, you have project managers, product managers, software engineers, test engineers, technical architects, systems engineers, and other people who all provide an area of expertise that the other people don't bring to the table. It's good for business to have someone give perspective of the Black experience, and it shouldn't come from just one Black person because we aren't all the same (which goes for any race or culture for that matter). With advanced technologies like facial recognition, how do we ensure you are testing all skin tones if your entire team is one skin tone? How do we ensure that when ChatGPT returns some information based on data that didn't include the Black experience, we don't release software where something was missed because it had a blind spot?

At the end of that conversation, my CTO's question was simple: "How do I get access to my Black technologists?" See, at his level, he never had interactions with the company's Black employees because we were all at the manager level or below. The way promotions happen is exposure! You have to be exposed to the people who are making the decisions about who to promote, and we were all hidden figures. When I asked multiple VPs to name five Black people in the organization, no one could because not only were there so few of us, but no one had exposure to executive leadership as well.

Because of this, I asked for his support to create an Employee Resource/Affinity Group specific to Black technologists. To take it a step further, instead of it being specific to our business segment, we made it enterprise-wide. The company was so big that not only did we not have exposure to executive leadership, but we also didn't have exposure to one another. During such a difficult time, we were all feeling alone and isolated, and we all needed one another for support. So, that year, I founded the Black Technologist Affinity Group and created a network that executives could tap into for ideas, feedback, and a talent pool. I created the safe space that not only I needed but that most others who were Black in the company needed as well.

I will never forget our first meeting when everyone was just so happy that they weren't the "only" on the video screen. We were able to have roundtable discussions with executives and get the exposure we needed. It was time to take away the excuse that there weren't enough of us in technology to promote. Because our numbers were (and are still) low, recruitment had to be targeted the same way we targeted women in tech. We had to go recruit at historically Black colleges and universities (HBCUs). We had to go to conferences specifically for Black technologists or organizations such as the National Black MBA Association and the National Society of Black Engineers. I remember being questioned as to why we would go recruit technologists at a business conference. I was eager to explain that most of us who want technology leadership roles have an undergraduate degree in technology but a master's in business, and, quite honestly, those are the type of people you should want as technology leaders. Those conversations were very thought provoking, and I kept being referred to as a senior manager. I had to make it clear that I was not in fact a senior manager, although I was doing senior manager–level work. A few months later, I was promoted.

From that year forward, I was the butterfly that fought its way to emerge from the chrysalis but was still sitting on the edge of the tree branch strengthening and fanning its wings. I continued to grow the affinity group. I continued to mentor and coach members of the network. I even finally found my own mentor who was actually a Black woman in the role I was trying to get to, and it was such a sigh of relief to have that. I continued to listen and be the voice for those who may still feel muted. In some people's eyes, I was flying, but in my own eyes, I was still sitting on that branch, flexing my wings, letting the world know that I was ready and willing to take flight when it came time.

FlutterBytz:

- When a butterfly starts to emerge from the chrysalis, the struggle and fight out of the chrysalis is an important part of the process. The struggle is how it strengthens its wings. Think about how many times we have struggled in life, and we didn't realize that it was a part of our process. There is also a point in time when the butterfly has emerged, but it appears that it's not ready to take flight. During that time, it is pumping fluid to its wings. So, when we think we aren't making progress or moving fast enough, take a moment to ensure your wings are strong enough to take flight. Don't rush the process!

CHAPTER 6

FIGHTING YOUR WAY TO FREEDOM

Emerging can be extremely painful in some cases. Your chrysalis phase can feel lonely and stagnant. It can involve feeling like there is a lack of movement, and, for those who feel like they have to be constantly moving toward something, this can be uncomfortable. This phase requires extreme patience. I thought that would be the hardest phase, but what I learned is that emerging is one of the most uncomfortable and difficult phases. You've spent an extended period of time in a place where although there is a lack of movement, you may have gotten comfortable being there. You may have begun to feel safe in your chrysalis, but you can't stay there. The fight could actually be that you are fighting to stay stagnant. Your old self and your new self could be at war with each other, or you may go through something so painful that you physically or emotionally feel like parts of you have died. This next part of my journey was just that. As part of my own personal healing journey, I had to go back to revisit the things that I had been hiding from. But this was a very necessary part of my process and often felt like a fight for my life.

Dealing with Grief and Loss

My life forever changed at the end of 2021. I lost my biological father, which put me through a pain that I wasn't prepared to cope with. Losing a parent is never easy, and this particular circumstance sent me through a range of emotions that would take an entire year for me to really learn to live with.

Let me provide some context. My father didn't raise me and wasn't a consistent figure in my life. He and my mother married young in the early '70s after my brother was born. I was born five years later, and by the time I was two, they had separated. Because of this, I had no real solid memories of their life together other than some not-so-great ones. In a nutshell, he struggled with drugs, and that prevented him from being the father that I really needed and wanted him to be. I was angry with him for many years. It took me well into my forties to learn to have empathy for him. I had to learn that his drug struggles did not equate to a lack of love for me or my brother.

The weekend of my forty-first birthday in 2016, I learned that he had fallen down and was in the hospital with a broken pelvis. The doctors also discovered he was in kidney failure, and cancer had been found in his bladder as well as his lungs. It wasn't looking good. They needed to get his kidneys stable before they could even address anything else, but I was told he was giving up. I got on a plane to Pittsburgh thinking it would be the last time I would see him. Something about my visit gave him the will to fight. My presence made him perk up, and we had a very heartwarming conversation where he apologized for not being the father I needed. It was the first time I had seen my father cry. Something about that conversation touched me and made me feel like maybe he really did love us.

After that weekend, he pulled himself together and fought for his life. He went to rehab for his pelvic break, started dialysis three days a week for the rest of his life, and began chemotherapy. The cancer was under control, and we spent the next five and a half years working on our relationship with the time we had left. It wasn't perfect. There were still times I would get angry and impatient with him, but I loved my father. My anger toward him was because I wanted him to love me the way that I needed him to love me instead of accepting the only love that he knew how to give me. He loved me the best way he could. Knowing that he experienced the struggles of being a fatherless Black man himself, in the inner city in a country that wanted the Black family to be broken up by making drugs readily available to either take or sell, and sometimes a bit of both, allowed me to have empathy toward my father and his own struggles in life. My father was one of many whose life was affected by drugs and the prison system, and it wasn't until I was in my forties that I understood his absence and how his presence may not have been the best thing for us.

At this point, in 2021, I called my father on his birthday at the end of September like I always do. I knew at some point his illness would end our time together, but no one is ever really prepared to accept that. Earlier that year, he was hospitalized, and I was told once again it wasn't looking good, but that was the fourth time he had pulled through, and we could turn off the false "this is it" alarm. After he was sent home, we talked for about an hour, and I noticed our conversations started to feel more final. There were more apologies and more "I lived the best life I could" comments. This conversation on his birthday was less upbeat. His mood felt defeated and tired. He told me he hadn't been feeling well, and for the first time, he admitted his cancer was spreading. I think it was denial, but I really didn't think things would turn for the worst so quickly.

A few days before Halloween, my aunt called with his doctor on the phone. This was the first time this had occurred, so I knew it must be it. The doctor informed me that my father was really sick, his organs were shutting down, and he was "transitioning." As his daughter, I was considered his next of kin even though my aunt and uncle were his caretakers. I was asked if I wanted to put him on a breathing tube when his lungs gave out or if I wanted to let him pass away. My heart sank! It's one thing to be told your father is transitioning, but it's a whole different feeling to have to be the one to make a decision to let him pass away. I could hear him saying he didn't want to go to a hospice or want a breathing tube, so I respected his wishes. I told him to hold on and that I would be there soon. Over the next day, I had the biggest internal struggle. My uncle told me that if I wanted to remember my dad the way he was the last time I had seen him earlier that year, then it was best that I didn't come. He told me the man lying in this hospital bed wasn't that person. I went through a flurry of emotions because in 2003, I watched his mother deteriorate from cancer. Only it was a lot worse because she didn't fight it for years. There was no preparation. One day she was walking to her car and lost control of the left side of her body and never regained it. A few months later, she was gone, and it completely shattered my heart. I'm sharing all of that to explain my turmoil. It took me a long time to recover from that, and I was adamant that I wasn't going to go to Pittsburgh to watch my father die. I just couldn't do it.

So the next day I decided to call my aunt via video call so that I could see my father for the last time, talk to him, tell him I love him, and consider it my goodbye. My aunt said he was in and out of consciousness, no longer talking much, and the doctors said he was pretty delirious. However, when they held the phone up and he opened his eyes to look at me, he perked up and said, "Hey! Where are you!?!?" My aunt started crying because she said he hadn't really been responding or reacting much, but something about my phone call helped him bounce back some. My father needed me, and at that point it wasn't about me and what I wanted. He was waiting for me, so I told him I would be there soon and to just hold on.

At that point, no one had really given me a timeline on how long he had to live. So that Saturday morning, I got on a plane to Pittsburgh with plans to return back to my home the next evening. I only intended to see him and say my goodbyes because, like I said, I did not want to watch my father die. I remember waking up that morning, and there was an eerie downpour of rain outside of my window. At this point in my life, I was very spiritually connected, and there were things I looked at around me as signs that I needed to pay attention to. To me, that rain symbolized the heavens opening up and my ancestors descending to take my father home, and it was time for me to prepare for that. So, I arrived at his side to see him connected to numerous tubes and machines. One machine was keeping his kidneys going, and I was told that if we removed that machine, he would pass away. Another machine was keeping his blood pressure up, and without that machine, he would pass away. He also had an oxygen mask over his face that was pushing air into his lungs, and although it wasn't breathing for him, it also was keeping him alive.

He tried to get up to hug and kiss me when he saw me, but I told him to just relax. I kissed his forehead and just held his hand. He loved jazz—he, my uncle, grandmother, and brother all played the piano, and I had many childhood memories of them playing during the times we did spend together. So, something made me pull out my phone and turn on a "Song for My Father," by Horace Silver, because it was one of the songs they used to play together. Through his pain, my father bobbed his head back and forth to the music with his eyes closed. At one point, I could see his hand moving beneath his covers as if he was playing the piano. He opened his eyes and whispered the best he could, "That's for you." Those were our last moments together. When the music ended, he started trying to pull his oxygen mask off and told me to take it off him. When I told him I couldn't and that he needed to keep it on, he said to me, "Yes, you can." He said he was tired and he wanted to go home, so I told him I would get the doctor.

The next few hours were the hardest of my life. The doctor came in and explained that he was never going to get better and that the machines were just prolonging his transition. He was never going home. So, my aunt, uncle, and I made the painful decision to let him go. In the movies when you see someone make these decisions, the person is in a coma or something terrible, but my father was in and out and awake, talking to me and listening to music. I know he was in pain and likely holding on for me, but I would live with the guilt of that decision for a year. I wasn't sure if he knew what turning everything off and going home really meant for him. I stepped out of the room while they turned everything off, but they sedated him before I had the chance to tell him I love him one last time—another pain I wasn't prepared for. For three hours, I watched his oxygen levels and heart rate drop and alarms go off that I would have nightmares about for months after. My brother called from Orlando, and I gave him the news that this was it. About an hour later, my daughter called for an update. While I was talking to her, his heart stopped while I held his hand. It was almost like he was waiting on them. Five hours after I walked into that hospital room, my father was gone. I didn't wake up that morning thinking that's how my day would go, and my life was different from that point on.

There's something about losing a parent that I wasn't prepared for. There's an indescribable pain. Even though our relationship was strained, I realized that this person was a part of me. There was a physical and spiritual connection because his blood runs through my veins. I literally felt like a part of myself died. I felt empty and lost. I felt like my heart beat a little differently. I felt tremendous grief. I couldn't watch a hospital show or a movie scene where someone died for months. The sound of a flat line on TV would immediately trigger me into tears that were uncontrollable. No one ever really explains the trauma that comes along with grief. Not only did I carry this guilt that I made a decision to kill my father, which I know wasn't really true, but the trauma of watching him die is a heavy thing to carry, and, quite honestly, I was never the same. It took about three months of grief therapy to get through it, where I also learned that I had post-traumatic stress disorder. I was in my chrysalis that I just wanted to stay in forever, but these events were pushing me out of it because I had transformed.

There was a secondary grief that I had to deal with—one that I really wasn't expecting. I have a really big family, and many of us are close. Things are good when times are good, but when times are bad, that's when I expected those close to me to be there to help me through it. I struggled for an entire year because, as the person who is always strong for others, people didn't know how to show up for me when I needed someone. I wasn't strong enough to even ask for help.

There was a confusion around the fact that my relationship with my father was strained and, therefore, maybe I shouldn't have been sad about him dying. I could understand someone's point of view around that, but at the same time I was grieving, and I didn't have the opportunity to really explain to others what I needed. I couldn't explain the trauma surrounding the circumstances of his death. Without talking to me, no one really knew what I was going through from taking him off life support, and I just shut down. I was just trying to get through my grief, and I had to without the people who I felt were closest to me.

Luckily, there were others like friends and other family members who stepped in and lifted me up. I want to be clear that this didn't mean I had anger toward the others, but there was extreme disappointment. It really wasn't about them; it was mostly about me trying to maneuver a new normal that would never be the same. I would never go back to the person that I was prior to my dad passing away, and it's hard for people who have not lost a parent regardless of the relationship to understand what it feels like when that parent is physically gone.

With this Butterfly Code, you can be in different phases for different things, and when it comes to my father passing away, I'm still slowly emerging. The caterpillar I was before this completely died along with him, and I'm still trying to figure out who I am supposed to be on the other side and if I'm even strong enough to fight myself out of it. Each year on the anniversary of his death, I still wake up emotional and not because I'm not at peace with him no longer being here but because I'm reminded of the trauma and the pain that day represented for me.

So, for anyone grieving, all I can say is that it's OK to not be OK some days. It's all a part of our process, and, one day, we'll emerge from it stronger. Different, but stronger. I'm happy to say that after some time, I was able to talk through that difficult time with some of my family members, and we were able to move past it. A part of that was my understanding that until someone walks through your fire, they can't begin to understand how much it burns and hurts.

The Importance of a Father's Love

I want to give a little more history about my father and how his death impacted me deeper than I would have imagined—in ways deeper than just dealing with his death.

I'll start at the beginning. I'm a Daddy's girl! Even though my parents separated when I was two, my dad was my very first love when it came to a man. However, I believe my life would have been much easier if I just never knew him versus him being in and out at various phases. I don't have many memories of living with him, but I can recall some tumultuous times between him and my mother. I can also recall some great and happy times when we would visit my grandmother's home where he lived, like when he would play the piano with my brother and uncle. My grandmother's house was a place filled with some of my most fondest childhood memories. But it was also a place where some of my disappointments with my father began.

I hoped if we were there, I would get the opportunity to see him. But those visits started being more of my brother and I trying our hardest to stay up late waiting for him to come home from wherever he was to spend time with us. Sometimes we were lucky; sometimes we'd have to see him the next day in the late afternoon when he finally emerged from the bedroom where he slept. It wasn't very long before he was back out the door, and we weren't sure when we'd see him again.

When I was nine, my father disappeared to Ohio where my uncle lived. Some weekends or summers, my grandmother would pack up the car and drive us up there, and once again, it was back to piano playing or cards and lots of laughs and love. We didn't have to stay up late to wait for my dad because my uncle kept him in line and made sure he was around to spend time with us. My uncle ended up getting married and starting a family and decided to move back to Pittsburgh, but my father didn't come with him. So it got harder to see or spend time with him. I didn't understand why he wouldn't come back, but I remembered that I was twelve when six years would pass before I saw him again. I was too young to really express how heartbreaking that was for me.

I recall one summer when I was getting ready to start high school and took a trip to Detroit with my uncle, aunt, and cousins to visit some family. My uncle told me we were going to stop in Ohio and that I would be able to see my dad. I was so excited because I missed him so much. I remember my uncle going to "look for" my dad, something I later learned that he did often. Eventually, he came back and asked me to come sit down with him. He then explained to me that I wouldn't be able to see my father because he was in jail. Again, my heart was shattered into a million pieces. I can still see myself sitting on the back porch crying. This is probably one of the hardest sections for me to write because I have to relive this harsh memory. I became a different person that day. I shut down inside. I built up a brick wall around myself for protection. I just couldn't take the hurt and disappointment anymore, and even though I loved that man with all my heart, it was easier for me not to. I convinced myself that day that I didn't.

Eventually, when I was old enough to comprehend, it was explained to me that my father had a drug addiction, and some of his behaviors started to make sense to me. The late nights out, coming home with bloodshot eyes, sleeping until who knows when the next day, and going right back out into the streets made more sense. I recalled a time when we were with him and he went into a pool hall in the middle of the winter in Pittsburgh and left us in the car. It felt like we were left for hours before he came back. I remember crying with my brother and feeling abandoned. It made sense that my mother needed to leave the marriage to protect us. I can't and don't blame her at all for that. I also learned that he had to leave Pittsburgh to protect his own life. Instead of me being understanding, it just made me more angry at him. I took it personally and felt like he didn't love us enough to not choose drugs over his family, not understanding that addiction is an illness and it wasn't that simple. So, I stayed behind my brick wall and kept any and every one from getting close to me for my own protection.

Even though I didn't see him after I turned twelve, he would call us here and there, and he always told us he loved us. It just didn't feel like love to me. My last long-distance phone call from him was from jail on my eighteenth birthday. It was just another normal call. I was happy to hear from him, but I had just gotten used to life without him. During that phone call, he told me that no matter what, he would be at my high school graduation. My mother told me not to get my hopes up, so I didn't. My life with my father taught me about not having expectations so that you won't be disappointed. But one thing I can say is that my father never made promises. He never told me he would be somewhere or do something and not show up. I never recalled sitting and waiting for him to pick us up and him not being there.

I completely forgot about that conversation and went on with life until the day I watched my family walk into my graduation. When I saw my grandmother, my father was there walking beside her. He had kept his word, and a flurry of emotions swept through me. I was ecstatic to see him but, at the same time, wanted to ask him where the hell he had been all of my life.

He was absent from the most crucial and critical times of my life up until that point, and that was when I needed him the most. Where was he to teach me about boys and how to protect myself from heartbreak? Where was he when I was going through my awkward phase and didn't know how to embrace my rounded teenage nose or full lips and I just needed him to tell me I was beautiful? Where was he when I started dating a guy who was a drug dealer so that he could tell me everything he knew about that lifestyle and what to stay away from? These were all the things that I wanted to scream at him, but instead, I held it in and was just grateful that he was there, and I could say that Daddy was home.

Unfortunately, Daddy wasn't really home. He was back in Pittsburgh, but from then until the time I graduated college and moved to Atlanta, he didn't really try to make it right. I can't recall there being many times when he would come looking for us or try to take us to dinner or lunch or just hang out. I would only see him if I went to visit my grandmother. He pretty much avoided us because he wasn't willing to hear us tell him how hurt we were by his absence. He kept trying to blame my mother saying she took us away from him and we would just lose it on him. So again, I stayed behind the brick wall and held firm that it was easier to not love him than to allow him to not love me the way I needed him. Then he did the ultimate heartbreak when one day he called me and asked me to borrow $100. I wasn't disrespectful because he was still my father, but I had a conversation with him that caused us not to talk for an entire year. Years went by, my daughter was born, and, for most of her life, the grandfather she knew of was my stepfather, who is an amazing man who luckily came into my life when I was sixteen. My brother got married, and our biological father didn't show up, and I just couldn't deal with him anymore. I honestly could take him or leave him. I made myself believe that I didn't care if he was alive or not because it was almost like he wasn't.

Things didn't turn around until he was diagnosed with cancer, and he decided he was going to fight after I showed up at the hospital. It was as if me coming there let him know that I actually did love him. In reality, I did, but I was afraid to face that. I am forever grateful that he decided to fight for the next six years because it gave me the opportunity to heal. We called each other more. We had more heart-to-heart talks. I learned about the real him. The truly ugly side of him.

The terrible things he had done in life and how him staying away from us was really for our protection. Protection from himself as well as the people who were trying to hurt him. He admitted that my mom was the love of his life, and after she didn't want to remain married anymore, he didn't feel like he had anything to live the right way for. He talked about his drug habits and his lack of having a father. The closest man to him was my uncle who had gone to the Vietnam War and left my father behind and how that affected him.

I can't say that it was all OK, but I learned to have empathy. I learned to not make his absence about me and tried to understand what he was dealing with in his own life as a Black man born in the '50s and having two children born in the '70s. I know how hard it was being a parent at close to thirty, so thinking about having a child at eighteen and another at twenty-three and then on the verge of divorce by the time he was twenty-five is a lot. So, I found a way to forgive him, not for him but because I needed it for me.

Two years before he passed away, he kept calling and urgently asking to come visit my brother and me in Orlando. He wanted me to help him buy a plane ticket so that he could fly down. I kept putting it off and ignoring his calls because honestly it was going to be a lot of work for me to make that trip happen. My father was already in kidney failure and had to have dialysis three times a week, so a weeklong visit would include lots of medical care that I just wasn't up to dealing with. I eventually respected his wishes after realizing he probably didn't have a lot of time left and just wasn't telling us. So, I flew to Pittsburgh to get him, and he spent the week of Thanksgiving with us. It was nice to have our father visit us in our homes for the first time in our adult lives, and it was nice to be able to cook for him during a holiday. We had never spent a holiday with him that I could recall. He liked fishing, so my brother got the chance to take him to the ocean for a fishing trip and spend some time with him that I know he really needed.

However, it was one of the most stressful weeks. As much as we probably needed that, I felt relieved when it was time to put him on the plane to go back home. I felt angry and resentful. Maybe it was selfish, but it was how I felt. I felt resentful that he had never taken care of me, but I had to take care of him. I felt angry that I had to drop everything and make accommodations for him to visit when he finally felt like it even though I probably needed him to make that visit.

Now let's fast-forward to the day he died. There I was again having to be the person to make decisions for his life when he was never my caretaker. I'm still grappling with the fact that I feel anger about that, and I don't know why. So, each year on the day of his death, I go through this extremely emotional day not because he's gone but because of the range of emotions that I had to deal with that day. I think there is still a part of me that feels like I never got what I needed from him before he died, and I never will. I remember standing at his casket in the cemetery, and one of my cousins who lived in Pittsburgh and was around my father more than I was said, "You were like my dad," and I remember my brother and I looking over at him and looking at each other as if we were both feeling how painful that was to hear. How could he have been like a father to someone else and not us? He lived in the same house with them for many years, so they had everyday access to him when we didn't. I listened to people speak at his funeral and talk about all these great and wonderful things about my father that I never got the chance to witness or experience. It was almost as if I didn't really know him at all. So, for anyone who doesn't understand how someone who wasn't extremely close to their father could grieve his loss so much and deal with so much pain, this is my version of that explanation.

What I'm most grateful for is that earlier that year when he had another close call and they didn't think he was going to make it, I had the hardest, most cathartic cry I had ever had about my father in my entire life. I recall speaking out loud in my living room that I wasn't ready for him to die and that I really did love my father with all of my heart. I was no longer afraid to love him. I understood that he loved me the best way he knew how and before he left this Earth, he was able to break that brick wall down so that I didn't have to live the rest of my life still hiding behind it.

I want you to take note that I'm talking about a brick wall and not cocoons or chrysalis. I can't say if or how my relationship with my father was part of my process. I don't know if anything in life could have prepared me for this part of my journey. I don't know if his absence was anything to evolve or transform from, but I did have to make a decision to emerge and face myself and what I was hiding from. I felt it was important to share that part of my story for anyone who may be struggling with the absence of their father. There are some things in life that just may not make sense, and I don't want anyone to feel like I'm saying that every terrible thing in life is meant to make you stronger. I wish I had my biological father in my life more. I needed him, and I still feel cheated, but I understand that for my own mental health, I had to allow myself to heal.

FlutterBytz:

- There is no timeline on grief. Do not allow someone to tell you how long you should or shouldn't grieve. Also understand that grief can include the trauma that may have surrounded the death of a loved one. Allow yourself to grieve in your own way and time. Understand that you will never be the same. You will never get over it but learn to live with it. This is one of the biggest examples of transforming and emerging as a different person.
- To people on the other side of grief who may not understand, please don't try to tell people how to feel. If you've never lost a biological child or parent, do not try to compare it with the loss of a grandparent or family member whom you haven't had some sort of physical connection to. It's different!

CHAPTER 7

TOTAL HEALTH—MIND, BODY, SPIRIT

I want to take some time to talk about taking care of your health. When I say health, I mean total health, which includes mental, emotional, spiritual, and physical. This could be for men or women, but I'm going to share some things about my health journey that were critical to my overall health. The reason I'm speaking about this is because, in order for us to emerge and take flight as a full version of ourselves, we have to address anything that may be weighing us down and hindering us from flying.

Here, I want to share about my journey with fibroid tumors. I had suffered from fibroid tumors for many years. During my doctor appointments, they weren't bothering me other than them just being there, so I was told to just leave them alone. My first fibroid tumor was discovered during my pregnancy with my daughter. It was nineteen years later before I finally had to take action. As someone dedicated to working on her career and being very ambitious about achieving goals, we often think we don't have the time to take out for ourselves.

In 2022, I started to notice that my stomach was getting very big. We had gone through a couple of years of COVID-19, working from home, being in the house, not moving as much, not really taking care of our health the way that we should, so I just assumed I had picked up weight. As I started trying to work out, eat better, lose weight, and do all kinds of exercises, nothing was taking my stomach down. I started noticing that my stomach was very hard, and my lower stomach was protruding out way more than it should and was pushing the rest of my stomach up. I noticed that I couldn't hold my bladder for long. I couldn't sleep throughout the night without having to get up to use the bathroom.

During my primary care visit, my doctor poked around on my stomach. This was a general checkup, and the first thing she asked me was if I had fibroids. She was very shocked, and she made a comment that she should not be able to touch my stomach and feel them. (I want to call out that I had recently switched to a new primary care doctor who was a Black woman, and I'll come back to why that's important later.) I told her I had been dealing with the fibroids but that my gynecologist told me if they weren't bothering me, I should just leave them alone. Her response was that I should get a second opinion.

My work life picked back up, and of course, I didn't prioritize getting a second opinion. But I felt like something intervened that caused me to. During the time that my annual gynecologist checkup was scheduled, a hurricane was moving through the area, and my doctor's office was going to close the day of my appointment. They told me to call the office to reschedule. I use that as an opportunity to make an appointment with a new doctor.

So, right after my forty-eighth birthday in January 2023, I made an appointment with a new gynecologist. When I walked in, I knew this office was kind of different because the ultrasound machine was right in the room where the doctor did the exam versus me having to go create another appointment with the imaging and wait for the results. Every time I had an ultrasound over the previous five years with the other doctors, the technician would be horrified with what they saw. So, I was always a little concerned when the doctor would call with the results and tell me that as long as nothing was bothering me, they would see me next year. This appointment was different.

During my exam, she calmly asked if I had children. I laughed because I knew that a hysterectomy was probably going to be recommended. I told her that I did have a child and she was turning nineteen. A few minutes later, the doctor came in, and she looked at my results. She mentioned that my stomach was about the size of being four to five months pregnant, it was not normal, and whoever had told me if they weren't bothering me to leave them were giving me incorrect information.

She asked me if I had lower back pain. I did, but I never thought that they were from the fibroids causing additional weight in my lower back. She asked me if I use the bathroom frequently, which I was. I thought being bothersome meant I was having heavy periods or pain, which I was not, but because I had an intrauterine device (IUD) that stopped me from having periods at all. She told me I had about five pounds worth of fibroids in my uterus. And although that may not seem like a lot, she told me to walk around with a five-pound weight all day every day and see how my back feels. She laid out some options that would be to remove the fibroids, with a high probability that they will probably return. At that point I would probably have to have yet another surgery to remove the fibroids again. She shared the option to have a hysterectomy that would include leaving my ovaries intact. This would give me the option to not go into menopause right away. I got worried because I thought a hysterectomy would need me to be out of work for eight weeks and off my feet. There was so much going on with work that it wasn't a good time for me to be out for eight weeks. She explained that now technology allows you to have the surgery laparoscopically and I would only need to have some small incisions they were going to go through with a robot to remove everything through the small incisions and that I could likely be back on my feet in about three weeks, although the total healing time would be six to eight. She referred me to a surgeon who also provided the same information, and by the next month, I was having the surgery.

Everyone's situation has to be based on what works for you and your own life and what's your best scenario. For me, I didn't need to keep my uterus anymore, so I was fine having a hysterectomy. As a matter of fact, there was a family history with fibroids, and I knew at some point it would become a problem. For some reason it was like taboo talking about having a hysterectomy or problems with your lady parts. But I made a decision to talk about it publicly as well as share it in this book because that year I learned that at least four people whom I knew were going through the same problems. We as women continue to suffer in silence and do not talk about family health, history, and things that we need to know about to take care of our own health and sometimes take our health into our own hands.

Let's circle back to my mention of having a Black doctor. I had heard that healthcare with Black women could be problematic and that we as Black women are not always treated the same. I really didn't think that was true because I had never experienced unfair treatment from doctors' offices. But it did make me angry to know that I had spent years dealing with these growing fibroids even though every year I ask the doctor what I should do. The moment I stepped into the doctor's office for a second opinion, as well as the surgeon's office, they both agreed immediately that my stomach should not be that big. I finally knew that I wasn't in the proper care.

So, I'm going to say to anyone reading this that whether it's fibroids or any other health condition, I know that we put our lives and our care in the hands of doctors whom we should trust, but listen to your body and don't be afraid to get a second opinion and to do what's best for you. Had I not had the surgery, I would've continued to suffer until it was an emergency.

It's more common than we think because we don't talk about it. Don't let your health get to the point that it's an emergency. If you have health insurance, take the time to get a yearly checkup. Make sure you're checking your blood levels, your A1C especially if you have diabetes in your family, check your cholesterol levels, and your blood pressure. If you're a man, get your prostate checked. Men and women should get colonoscopies done. We have to take the time to take care of ourselves before it's too late, and if you do have health insurance, most of the time preventative healthcare is covered 100 percent.

Get your yearly gynecologist appointments taken care of. Get your yearly regular health checks. Get your mammograms every year. I also had a mammogram issue that I had to get taken care of as well. With my very first mammogram, something was found, and I had to get a biopsy, but all was well. So, I just wanted to dedicate this section on taking care of your physical health and making sure that you're taking care of yourself. And this is a part of strengthening your wings. I couldn't soar, and I couldn't fly by carrying all that extra baggage with health issues. The things that were weighing me down were preventing me from becoming the healthiest version of myself. So, strengthening your wings also includes making sure your total health is in alignment.

****

Let's transition to mental health. What many people may not know about me is that when I was twenty-five, I went through a bout with depression. It was a very dark time for me, and it was something that I just couldn't understand. I felt that I was living my best life. I did everything that I was supposed to do right up until that point in my life. I graduated from college with my technology degree, I had a great job in Atlanta, I was in a great relationship that hadn't yet turned toxic, and we had just purchased our dream home. I had everything I wanted and needed, but I went through weeks of not wanting to get out of the bed. I went through days where I couldn't stop crying, and I couldn't figure out why. I didn't have anything to really be sad about. My life was great, so why was I so sad?

I started going to therapy, and, ultimately, I had to get on medication for about a year. Therapy was another one of those taboo words. We were supposed to go to church and pray through our problems, but that's the reason why so many of us are walking around mentally unhealthy. I didn't know what anxiety was growing up. Depression was something that probably ran deep within my family, but we never talked about it. If I think about it, it makes sense that depression would run deep. If we start looking about the things that Black families have had to carry and deal with and just get over it with a smile on our faces, eventually we'll break.

The reality was that even though I had everything that I wanted, I didn't have everything that I needed. I needed my father in my life. His absence and not being there contributed to my self-esteem and self-worth. I felt like if my own father didn't love me, who would? I later understood that my father actually did love me with all of his heart and that his absence had nothing to do with his lack of love for us but his struggles with substance abuse. Remember that brick wall I talked about? It wasn't actually protecting me as much as I thought it was. I was just hiding behind it, and eventually, depression kicked in and took me down. I could talk about all of the things that contributed to my depression, but I'd rather have this book focus more on the positive than all of the not-so-great things that have happened in my life.

I just want to take a moment to say that your mental health is important. Take care of it. Don't run from it. Go to therapy! Meditate, pray, and go talk to a professional. It's OK. Don't continue to drown and not ask for help. We can't always do it on our own. We can't always be strong through everything. If you are in your chrysalis and it's just too much, it's OK to ask for help sometimes. Ultimately you will have to make the decision to emerge, but maybe you need a little extra help to strengthen your wings and fly.

FlutterBytz:

- **It is sometimes hard to emerge if there are things weighing you down mentally, emotionally, and/or physically. Take the time to get your total health in order.**
- **It's OK to not be OK sometimes. Allow yourself to feel and address the feelings versus trying to mask them. This will allow you to heal completely instead of putting a bandage on the wound.**

STEP FIVE

TRANSCEND AND SOAR:

THIS IS WHERE YOU ARE MEANT TO BE!

Now you're free and the world has come to see just how proud and beautiful you are. Black Butterfly, sail across the waters. Tell your sons and daughters what the struggle brings.

—"BLACK BUTTERFLY," DENIECE WILLIAMS

CHAPTER 8

DREAMING BIG FROM THE SKY

Seven years after our first Disney Cruise and promising my daughter that we would sail every year, we were on our twelfth, and I was reflecting while looking out at the ocean and clear blue skies. I had been on all four of Disney's current ships and several different itineraries. We'd sailed to the Bahamas numerous times, the Eastern Caribbean, and the Western Caribbean, and this trip was a ten-night Southern Caribbean trip that I had the blessing of being able to take my parents with us. I was able to take my brother with me once, friends, and other family. I'd been able to sail twice and sometimes three times per year because I was put in the financial position to do so. At that moment, I thought I had made it! That life could get no better. Two weeks prior, I had launched some technology in California where I had the chance to take my daughter with me during the trip. Each evening after work, I returned to my room on the Club Level of a five-star hotel and would sit with my daughter on the balcony and admire the view of the mountains in the distance. It was her first trip to California, and it gave her the opportunity to see just how hard her mother worked and how she contributed to some amazing things with technology. At the time, it was one of the best summers we had ever shared together.

I had no idea that two years later, I'd be back. She was fifteen and had just finished her freshman year in high school. She was studying the Japanese language and culture, and I was wrapping up an eighteen-month-long technology project launching in Tokyo as well as another technology project in California. It was launch time, and my schedule consisted of spending one week in California and then two weeks in Tokyo with a one-week break in between. I didn't think twice about buying her a plane ticket to Los Angeles accompanied by a round-trip ticket to Tokyo so that she could come along with me for work. We spent an amazing time in California back at that same five-star hotel. During the day, I launched the project, and, in the evenings, I got to have some fun with my daughter after I finished. She was old enough at that point to hang out and explore on her own during the day.

When that week ended with a successful launch, we flew to Tokyo for a weeklong vacation before I started my two weeks of work there. Although I had been to Tokyo about eight months prior for a week of meetings and project planning, I didn't get the chance to really explore. My daughter was aspiring to be an animator and also had a love for Japanese anime. At that point I was using technology to create immersive experiences and what better way to help her study the language and culture than to immerse ourselves in it for three weeks. We explored all over the city, ate different types of foods and drinks, visited temples, prayed for blessings, shopped, and everything else we could think of. We stayed at a hotel right across from Tokyo Disney Resort and had direct access to the Maihama train station, so each day we would take the train and explore.

Our first stop was Akihabara where my daughter was lost in the land of Japanese anime. We walked around for hours on floors upon floors of art, figurines, and comic books. The second day we went to Harajuku and strolled Takeshita Street. We stopped into a cat cafe and an owl forest. We had lunch before going over to the Meiji Shrine and being amazed with its wonder. On the way back, we stopped at Odaiba for some shopping and for my daughter to take pictures with the giant Gundam outside. The next two days we explored Tokyo Disneyland and Tokyo Disney Sea and were simply amazed by the beauty of those parks. We finished the week by exploring Shibuya Crossing, shopping on Cat Street, and exploring the Senso-Ji Temple.

After my week off, I spent the next two weeks rolling out the technology project along with my team. I got to witness how our project impacted and improved the guest experience, and I contributed to that success. I was a long way from home, and I was an even longer way from where I had started.

The point of sharing this is to say that I was no longer dreaming big in small places. I now dream big in big places to go even bigger places. I dream big sitting out in the middle of the ocean thinking about when and where we will go next. I dream big on plane rides to Asia. I speak my goals, dreams, and desires out into the universe, and I don't worry about how and when they will come true. I just have faith that they will. It wasn't about winning the lottery so that I could take my child on a dream vacation. It's about speaking and praying for the desires of your heart and believing it will come true if you are faithful and have faith.

I was literally thousands of miles away from my small neighborhood in Pittsburgh, Pennsylvania, where I once as a young child dreamed of bigger things for my life. God had taken me places that were too big for me to even imagine for myself. You see, it doesn't matter where you are or what your circumstances are. I am a believer and living proof that you can dream big and go after your goals. When I reached that version of myself, I thought I had made it but only to learn that I was just getting started. There was still so much more growth, transformation, and even some struggles that I would still have to face. But my life kept elevating up to the point that one day my daughter said to me, "Mom, you're no longer a butterfly. You don't flutter, you soar! You're resilient. You've been through so much that I had no idea it was even happening in our lives. It's like you're a phoenix that rose from the ashes."

The World Is Yours!

One day I was looking at a picture of my daughter standing in front of the castle in the Magic Kingdom wearing a Princess Tiana dress and a tiara. She was seven years old at that time, and it was our first Christmas in Orlando. We had been in Orlando for only four months at that point. Not knowing what to expect, I embarked on a journey that my daughter called "an adventure."

I remembered standing in the Magic Kingdom that morning that had no way of knowing the transformation that I would go through. I had no idea of knowing how far this journey would take me. Looking at that picture made me realize that I had a daughter who was able to say that she grew up in Disney World because we lived so close. She would be able to say that Halloween would be celebrated collecting candy and watching parades at Mickey's Not So Scary Halloween Party or on a Disney cruise ship. The winter holidays would consist of taking the monorail to the different Disney resorts to see the holiday decorations and gingerbread houses, Mickey's Very Merry Christmas Party where we would do the Cupid

Shuffle with Pluto and Goofy while drinking hot chocolate and eating cookies, or better yet on another Disney cruise where we would get to see Castaway Cay all decorated and festive.

Random staycations at Disney resorts just to get away from the house for a day or two would become routine. Getting home from work and running over to EPCOT to watch Sheila E., Chaka Khan, Kenny G, or Boyz II Men perform at the Food and Wine Festival would become a part of life. Strolling around the Flower and Garden Festival on a relaxing spring Sunday would become normal. This journey wasn't just a job, but it had become a new and amazing lifestyle.

Being able to witness all of these technology launches would also become a part of her story and journey that she shared with her mother as a child and teenager. Her story would have a very different beginning than mine, but I knew she would have to go through her own transformation as well. Some of it I will be there with her to help her through, but some of it she will have to endure on her own. My hope is that I can be an example of her knowing she will come out on the other side stronger. What I also didn't know the day she took that photo at seven years old is that she would develop into an amazing artist with the ability to draw, animate, shoot films, and do photography. She would sometimes play a little piano or guitar on the side.

I began to think that maybe, just perhaps, my journey and my story were always meant to set the stage for hers. As a creative, she had the opportunity to grow up with creativity all around her. My hope is to continue to be a motivator and inspiration to others as an example.

The Middle Passage—My Ancestors' Wildest Dream

In 2021, I had the opportunity to be on the technology delivery team of a new build out of a cruise ship, and in 2022, when the ship was complete, I had the opportunity to fly to Germany and be on the sailing that would bring the ship over to Florida. Those twelve days would serve as a dry run to make sure all the technology was in place and working properly before its first sailing with paying customers. Since it was the summertime and it was the final summer with my daughter before she went off to college, I was excited to bring her along with me just as I had done with every other big launch. It was our first time in Europe and our first time on a transatlantic sailing. We spent a few days in Germany as I met the team there to assist with application training. We were then out to sea for four days before a one-day stop in Portugal. We had the opportunity to walk around and explore, do some shopping, and enjoy a meal at a restaurant close to the port. We took in the beautiful architecture, and it was just a great feeling to once again share this experience with my daughter since the past few years had limited travel because of COVID-19.

We left Portugal and prepared ourselves for the five days at sea that would be required to get us to the Bahamas. At the end of our third day at sea, I can still remember how rocky the ship was. I remember sitting on the verandah of our room and seeing how dark the ocean was. It wasn't the beautiful blue water that I loved to look at. The sun had set, and other than the lights from the ship, you couldn't see anything but huge waves crashing up against the ship. I hardly ever get sick on cruises, but that evening I ended up throwing up because the ship was rocking so hard. I had a moment when I started to feel like I just wanted to get off, and I didn't know how I would survive one more day being out on that ocean.

Suddenly, something very spiritual and humbling washed over me. My daughter who was sitting next to me looking at the same ocean quietly says, "We're on the Middle Passage, Mom. You know, the slave ships left from Portugal." I immediately pulled myself together and started to reflect on what that really meant. I was sitting there on the tenth deck of a big fancy cruise ship complaining about being nauseous when my ancestors who were kidnapped and chained together at the bottom of a slave ship, not able to move and likely throwing up on themselves, had to endure so much worse. I looked out at the waves that were crashing up to at least the fourth deck and thought about those that jumped into that ocean to their death. There was no way anyone could survive those waves.

I got emotional. We sat quiet for a while, and if she wasn't with me, I wouldn't be sharing about the sounds we heard out there: the sound of a constant humming and random high-pitched squeals every so often. I would just look over at her to make sure I wasn't crazy, and she would just keep looking forward and say, "I heard it too, Mom." Was it whales? I don't know. Was it dolphins out there at the same time with the whales? I don't know. But it was a very spiritual and emotional experience for me.

There I was sitting there as the only Black person on the technology team on that ship as a senior manager. My life took on a different meaning that day. I had lost my father a few months prior, and I was just settling into the thought of him living on through me. But I reflected a lot deeper that day.

My grandmother was born and raised in Clarksdale, Mississippi. Everything I had ever seen or heard about Mississippi was horrible when it came to Black people. It was a place I never wanted to visit based on movies and things I had read about it. When I asked how my great-grandfather ended up in Pittsburgh, where he eventually brought his entire family including his parents and siblings, I was simply told he migrated there to work the steel mills. That was the easy answer. That was the less horrible version that a young kid could easily wrap their mind around. No one wanted to talk about how the Jim Crow Era had forced many families to flee as part of the Great Migration. As I got older, my father shared some of those not-so-great stories about my family who had passed on and how my great-grandfather had often told them to never go back down there. So, there I was sitting on that verandah reflecting on what my great-grandfather had to do in order to make a better life for his family—how he had the fight in him to make a better way for his family. If it hadn't been for him, I would not be sitting on that verandah with my own daughter carrying on their legacy as a technology leader on a cruise ship on the same path our ancestors left Africa. My relationship with my father was rocky, but my relationship with my grandmother and the rest of his family was always strong. I got so much clarity that night. I had peace with the fact that even if we didn't have the relationship that I had hoped, I was meant to carry on this bloodline, and this bloodline was part of where I got my strength.

It began to make sense to me why I was such a fighter. My father was a fighter. My grandmother was a fighter. I sat on that verandah that night and knew that I was my ancestors' wildest dreams, and I felt the biggest sense of pride and accomplishment. Ironically, we made it to the Bahamas on Juneteenth, and when I walked off of that ship in Florida, I was a different person. I felt like I had emerged and was flying high. I had transcended so much adversity that was not only my own but the adversity that had been passed down from generation to generation, and I knew that I couldn't stop. I couldn't give up. I had to keep going because my ancestors needed to live on through me and my daughter.

That was my moment! That was the moment that I felt like I had made it through each of these phases and I could spread my wings and proudly fly. At the end of that trip, I found the courage to step off the branch I had been sitting on and fly. It was time! It was time to tell this story. It was time to use this book as an inspiration to others that no matter the circumstances, we can grow, and we can evolve, transform, and emerge.

I sometimes feel like maybe my wings aren't strong enough and I took flight too soon. I sometimes get exhausted and tired because of some of the things that I am still carrying around or struggling with. But during those times, I find somewhere to rest and reset until I can fly again. What's important is that I did the work and went through all of the phases that I needed in order to get my wings and fly.

I hope these pieces of my journey relate to you in some way and are able to push through your own growth, evolution, and transformation. But I also want to make it clear that you can go through these cycles multiple times or be in multiple phases based on different things in your life. Professionally, I feel like I'm flying, but sometimes personally, I'm not. It's during those times that I give myself grace and take a break. An amazing thing about butterflies is that when they land and move from flower to flower, they are pollinating, allowing flowers to reproduce. Become a pollinator when you get your wings by inspiring and helping others grow who may be able to relate to your journey.

FlutterBytz:

- The journey from caterpillar to not just a butterfly but also to a butterfly that can fly and soar is a long process that you can't rush. The most important thing is to understand where you are in the process and the lessons that you are meant to learn during each phase.
- Keep pushing forward, growing, and developing until you are ready to take flight. It may start out as a flutter, but keep going until you can soar. If for some reason you crash and burn, just rise up out of those ashes and be reborn again like a phoenix.
- It won't be easy—it will get uncomfortable and sometimes seem painful, but when you finally get your wings, I hope you can look back and feel like it was all worth it.

SUMMARY

Now that you have gone through the phases with me, let's take a look back at the full Butterfly Code in hopes that you can apply it to your own life.

The Butterfly Code:

- Preparation: You must crawl before you can fly. Take advantage of your time on the ground. A caterpillar and a butterfly have two different vantage points. In the sky, you can't see all the little things that are on the ground, and once you're able to fly, you are less likely to spend time on the ground. Learn all that you can during your crawl stage. A caterpillar has to prepare itself for the chrysalis and so must you. Trust the process and find joy in the journey.
- Evolve: You aren't meant to stay a caterpillar. In order to become the full version of yourself, growth is necessary. In most cases, growth requires changes and may result in a complete metamorphosis of who you are now into who you are meant to be. Just as a baby must physically go through different stages of growth to become a fully grown adult, we will go through different mental and emotional phases as we are growing

into who we are meant to be. Be OK getting uncomfortable in order to grow. You aren't meant to stay where you are. Trust the process and embrace the journey.

- Transformation: Embrace change while being still in your chrysalis. Sometimes isolation and stillness are necessary during your growth period. A caterpillar goes into a chrysalis or cocoon and stays there by itself for a set period of time during its transformation. In your own journey, you may have to walk your path by yourself or be still for a period of time. It may be lonely, it may be uncomfortable, it may even be scary, but know that there will come a time when you will come out on the other side, the version of yourself that you are supposed to be.
- Emerge: Strengthen your wings. As a butterfly emerges from the chrysalis, the movement and the struggle are what make the butterfly stronger. Sometimes we may feel like we are in a battle or a fight with something that we are going through in life. During these times, stop and think about where you are in life. Is this struggle symbolizing something that will make you stronger in the end? As you break out of your chrysalis, your struggle is what will allow you to emerge as the new version of yourself, but you have to move. When it's time, move!
- Transcend and Soar: This is where you are meant to be! When the time comes, you will be ready to soar. Once you get to the point where you feel like you are flying, you will look back over your journey and realize that many of the things you have gone through were so that you can grow, evolve, transform, emerge, and eventually take flight. Be who you are born to be! Then share your journey with others.

You've survived, now your moment has arrived. Now your dream has finally been born. Write your timeless message clear across the sky. So that all of us can read it and remember when we need it. That a dream conceived in truth can never die. Butterfly!

—"BLACK BUTTERFLY," DENIECE WILLIAMS

ADDITIONAL FLUTTERBYTZ

This chapter isn't exactly going to tie into one particular butterfly phase, but they are the small pieces of information or small stories that I call FLUTTERBYTZ. This is a word or term I created that means a small piece of information (a byte such as the technical term) that will help you fly (Flutter).

Get Your Money Honey—Generational Wealth

This may or may not have anything to do with a butterfly, but can we talk about our money for a moment? I heard a term during a panel from Caroline Wanga, who was the CEO of *Essence* magazine.

She referred to many of us as "first generation corporate Americans." What that means is that there are many people who are working in corporate America as the first people in their families. We didn't or don't have someone to provide us a blueprint on how to maneuver climbing the corporate ladder.

I wish I had known in my twenties and thirties what I learned in my late forties when it came to understanding your worth. When you get to a point in life where your salary is well beyond what most people in your family ever imagined for themselves, they will tell you not to rock the boat and be grateful for that good job. It's very reminiscent of "master has been good to us so don't upset him." Here's the thing: no one has given you anything—you've earned it. You've worked twice as hard, did the work, educated yourself, and earned whatever you needed to in order to be qualified for the position that you are in. You are in that position because your credentials and qualifications placed you there.

Therefore, make sure you know what you are worth and should be paid. Understand the words "bonus eligible" if there are long-term incentives tied to your position. If you don't know what long-term incentives are, find you a mentor who is comfortable helping you determine what your worth is.

I want to quickly address anyone who may be reading this who isn't affected by the gender pay gap. How can you be an ally? If you see something, say something! If you have control over how people get paid in your organization, please take a look at the differences in salaries between men and women as well as people of color and non-people of color. I know a number of different factors go into salaries, but please make sure you aren't contributing to the problem, and if you have the ability to rectify something, do so. The gender pay gap is a real thing!

One year, as I was testing out my Butterfly Code Framework, I had a weekend retreat with seven of my close friends. It was the first time I had brought this group of Black women together, and everyone didn't know one another. Some of us were in technology and some weren't. The idea was for all of us to be around like-minded women, set goals for ourselves at the start of the year, and hold one another accountable. One of my good friends was in banking, and it was the first time she was around my other friends who were doing very well financially. It inspired her! She decided she wanted more for herself and wrote a goal that she would have a better job that year.

Well later that year, she got a job offer making significantly more than what she was making per year, but it would require her to move to another state. She stepped out on faith, took the job, and relocated. Ultimately, she hated the state that she moved to and, after a year, applied for jobs back in Florida. She ended up getting an offer from a bigger bank and getting yet a bigger jump in salary and had the confidence to negotiate her salary to even more. In a year's time, she doubled her salary because she learned her worth and the art of salary negotiation.

I'm sharing this story to say learn your worth and get your money, honey! We are leaving too much money on the table. Before you take an offer or leave your current job, make sure you are comparing things like pensions, 401(k), tuition reimbursement if you plan to go back to school, bonus, long-term incentive, and other company perks. Understand your total package and use your networks and mentors to help make decisions. Surround yourself with people who are like-minded and want to help see you grow as well.

Let me talk a little bit about generational wealth. I'm no expert at it, and it's not something I've been blessed with, either. Most of us are just one generation into having salaries in the six-figure range. So, the idea of making a way for our families to have wealth that we can pass down from generation to generation is foreign to us. When we talk about legacy, what would you want your legacy to be? It's an ugly truth many Black families in America help create generational wealth for others and were never compensated for it. It's also an ugly truth that some Black families in America created a way to have generational wealth, and it was taken away from them through various means that were hidden from history books.

So, I encourage you all to take some financial literacy classes. Make sure you have a life insurance policy that not only covers your funeral costs but also leaves something for your family to thrive when you are no longer here. Invest in real estate. Own your home. Understand what home equity can provide to you. Learn about other investment strategies. I was guilty of just letting my savings sit in a bank barely collecting interest. I had no idea that banks actually take your money and make their own investments with it and make money off your money. Learn how to make your money work for you. I'm still learning about trusts and such, so I won't really try to talk about it, but the point of this all is to make sure you learn ways to leave something or pass something along to your family after you are gone. That first starts with making sure you are getting paid what you are worth.

The Glass Ceiling and the Eleventh Checkbox

I want to get real for a moment about the glass ceiling. Let me circle back to the 3 percent of Black women in technology that I learned about in 2015. In 2023, that number had not changed. In 2023, there were still less than 10 percent of Black people in technology within the United States. The number of women in technology overall had grown to 27 percent, which meant we were doing the work to get more women into technology careers.[4] I could see firsthand how we were making a difference getting more people of color into technology

4 National Center for Women & Information Technology, "By the Numbers," accessed March 29, 2024, https://ncwit.org/resource/bythenumbers/.

fields. We were recruiting at HBCUs, and we were going to conferences targeted at Black talent in technology. I had seen more Black interns and new hires into the company than I had ever seen before. But let me tell you where the problem lies. Companies are creating a revolving door. I want to be sure that I say "companies" because this is not a problem with just one company. We are targeting entry level but not growing those who are already ten- to twenty-five years into their careers and have not had the opportunity to climb the ladder or grow. So, they leave the field for a tech-adjacent role just to earn that director or VP title. But let me tell you why this doesn't help your growth.

Let's start with understanding job categories. A director of software engineering isn't the same as a director of product management or a director of program management. The same goes for managers and senior managers. I had to learn that the hard way, when I took a senior manager position that was considered program management and no longer software engineering. No one explained to me that I was changing job categories and how my total compensation was impacted by that decision. Luckily, I got that rectified when I moved back into a software engineering role because I quickly learned that program management really wasn't where my heart was.

Let's take this a step further. A director of diversity, equity, and inclusion (DEI) is a very different job category from a director of, let's say, finance. Why am I telling you this? Because once we decide we want to get to an executive level, we start title chasing, and sometimes that title chase can be career limiting or make you completely miserable because it's not the role you really wanted but you settled for the title. You also might not be getting the salary you are qualified for because you removed yourself from the software engineering job family just to get a title.

I brought up DEI because that's where some people of color are encouraged to go sometimes. I'm passionate about DEI in technology, but I don't want it to be my full-time job because I'm a technologist. That's what I am educated in; that is where my twenty-five years of experience is, and that's the ladder I want to continue to climb. But I can't tell you how many times I've been told I'd be good in a DEI role, and I should maybe apply for an open position. There is absolutely nothing wrong with being in a DEI role if that's where your goals are. There is nothing wrong with being in program management or portfolio management if that's where your goals are. But if your goal is to climb the engineering ladder in software, data, or any other engineering job category, stand your ground and keep chiseling away at that glass ceiling. Don't give up! We've worked hard at this, and it's time for us to have a seat at the tables that we keep being told we aren't ready for.

When we leave, we are impacting that 3 percent. We're coming into the field, but then we leave it because we are exhausted from the upward battle associated with the climb. I won't give up because I know how many people are watching me for inspiration, and giving up would discourage so many people. So even though I didn't sign up for my career to be an inspiration and role model for others, I know that it is.

Now let's talk about the eleventh checkbox. Leaders and hiring managers, we have to stop putting the eleventh checkbox on us! This means that if the requirements are 1–10, then the requirements should be 1–10 for everyone. But what we often find is that John Doe only has 1–5, and that's considered acceptable when I may have 1–9 or even 1–10, but you've added an eleventh box that only I have had to check. Some people call this moving the goal post. Every year someone finds some additional reason to tell you that you aren't ready.

That's a hard pill to swallow as you watch all of your peers around you get promoted—some with less experience than you, and some who were still in middle school when you were earning your master's degree. Again, we're not asking for a handout. We aren't asking for special treatment. We're not asking anyone to hire someone just because they are Black because that's a recipe for disaster. What we are asking is that if we are in fact qualified, we aren't passed over because we are Black. For leaders reading this who know that you were offered an opportunity knowing that you weren't fully qualified for it, I just ask that you keep that in mind when you are considering someone who may be sitting in front of you who doesn't check all the boxes that you didn't either. And please, I beg you, please don't put an unqualified person in a role just because they are Black. It's not setting that person up for success, and quite honestly, we are going to feel like that one person will make us all look bad when that's not what they signed up for.

If we keep this up, we will just keep creating a revolving door. There are other opportunities out there for us, and sometimes to support our families or with the knowledge that the only way to move is to leave the company or take a position in a different job category, we simply just have to do what we need to do. Many are choosing to branch out and start their own companies with the years of knowledge and experiences they've gained, and that's OK, too.

Before I end this section, I have one last thing to say. Dear Black people: We are not one another's competition! If you make it to the top, make room for those you have mentored and/or sponsored. If you aren't mentoring and sponsoring someone who looks like you, please do so. We shouldn't have to compete and have this mentality that there can only be one. We are tired of being the only. There can be more than one of us on a team.

Dear other people: Please don't make us one another's competition. There is a tremendous amount of pressure on us when we are an "only." As I mentioned earlier, when we are in manager levels and above, we feel like we must be successful on behalf of all of the Black people on Earth. It's such a heavy burden to carry. It's a big reason why I don't want to ever carry the burden of being the first of anything.

Dysfunction and Toxicity

I want to take a moment to address dysfunction and toxic energy that could surround you. This could be friends, family, work, or anything that impacts your life. This is going to touch on two of the codes: one being you aren't meant to stay a caterpillar and the second is your alone time in your chrysalis.

I'm going to start with dysfunctional family and friends and what codependency can sometimes look like. I want to be clear that I'm not saying anything against large, loving families or ones that can appear to be loving but have pockets of dysfunction. When you're in an environment that you've grown up in and that's all you know, you don't always see that some of the behaviors in your family or friend circles can be abusive, toxic, or dysfunctional.

I'm not talking about being physically abusive here—I'm talking about mental or emotional abuse. When you begin to grow and change into the person that you are supposed to become, sometimes there needs to be a separation from what you used to be and what you used to be could have been a participant in a dysfunctional or toxic situation. And when you begin to separate from that, it's one of the hardest things you'll ever have to do because you never want to separate yourself from your family or cause division but sometimes those constructs are blocking you from your growth.

For example, while I was in my marriage, I didn't understand that it was toxic. I didn't understand or even know what mental and emotional abuse was. I was just in this ten-year situation of what I thought was love. I endured so much pain because you're taught not to give up on people and to stick things out. You're taught that your family is everything, and you hold on to that no matter how you may be treated. The moment you decide that's not OK for you anymore, you become the problem. I remember my ex-husband telling me that I was on a high horse when I decided that this was no longer enough for me anymore and that I wanted a better life. Like how dare I want peace! How dare I set boundaries for what's acceptable for my own life! When I did leave, I felt lost for a while. Even though I wanted to be free from what I was in, it was all I knew for ten years. The road to reprogram myself to love myself enough to not accept the behavior was a long and hard one, and I was sometimes encouraged to maybe go back by those who felt dysfunction and toxic relationships were normal.

You aren't meant to take everyone with you on the journey that you're supposed to go, and it's heartbreaking. It's heartbreaking when the people that you've known and been close to your whole life have to take a back seat to your growth and your journey. A lot of times we want to do things for the sake of others, and we want to do things to be able to bring them along with you, when in reality, the first thing you have to do is leave them behind, pave the way for yourself, and allow room for them to follow if they want to. We have to be willing to accept that some people may not want to come along or follow you on your journey. We also have to be willing to accept that some people may not want you to succeed in your journey. There may be some people in your circle who may try to stop your growth, block your growth, or pull you back to what they know and the only thing they're used to. That's why the alone time in your chrysalis is one of the hardest phases you'll ever have to endure. It's painful, it's lonely, and it's heartbreaking, but when you come out on the other side, you will be so free.

As I explained, everyone doesn't make it to become a butterfly. Everyone may not want to become a butterfly even though it's totally necessary for their survival, and we must accept that. In addition, people have to evolve on their own time and terms. We can't force people or rush them through the process because we're ready and we can't be angry or upset with them because they aren't. You must either meet people where they are or leave them where they are. It doesn't always mean that you have to leave people behind who aren't in the same phase or cycle as you, but we have to be cognizant of the fact that someone may not be in the same space as you. At that point, we must make a decision on if we want to help them get there, on their terms and time, or go on with our lives until they are ready to meet you where you are.

The most important thing I can tell you is that you can't go back. Once you evolve and transform, you aren't the person you used to be, and you're going to painfully feel like you don't fit into what and who you used to be because it's not you anymore. It became so freeing to me to finally say that's no longer me and I am not going to try to change who I am to fit in with who I used to be to make people comfortable. If someone isn't happy with my evolution and transformation, that's their problem, not mine.

To those on the other side of this, let me help explain why you shouldn't take this personally. When someone is on a healing journey from something that may be similar to a situation that you are currently in, your life can be triggering to them. For example, if I'm healing from a mentally, emotionally, and/or physically abusive relationship, but you are in one and every conversation we have is about your abusive relationship, it can be triggering to me as I am pulled back into reliving my own abuse. So, if a person decides that they can't sit in your dysfunctional or toxic situation with you, it's not personal toward you but critical to their own healing process. Until a person is fully healed and can use their own experiences to help you through yours comfortably, they may have to step away and leave you behind for a while. Give them grace, and allow them to make it through their own healing before they can be there for you.

I'm sharing this because we have been programmed to just deal with life no matter what. We accept abuse from family sometimes just because they are family. Meanwhile, if they weren't family, we'd never deal with these people again. So, instead of teaching one another to accept the behavior out of love, why don't we try to change the narrative to being a better family member? Let's stop the "hurt people, hurt people" commentary and treat people the way you want to be treated. If you are hurt, address the person who hurt you and let them know it's not and was never OK instead of taking your pain out on someone else. Let's stop accepting dysfunctional behavior as normal and break some of these cycles so that we can thrive in loving environments instead of toxic ones.

In closing on this topic, if you are the toxic or dysfunctional one, I encourage you to address your pain and hurt so that you aren't passing it along or creating dysfunction in your own families, friendships, or work environment.

Peace and Positivity

On the other side of dysfunction and toxicity is peace and positivity. I try my best to stay away from negativity and toxicity. I am a true believer and example of how changing how you think and what you say can completely change your life. Starting in 2011, when my life took a turn for the better, I started thinking differently and making sure I said more positive words of affirmation daily. Many of the great and amazing things that started happening in my life were because I started thinking I could achieve certain goals. I wrote them down and spoke them out loud almost daily. I started using a guided journal to write and think about them, and it's one of the reasons I created my own guided journal and notebooks for others to be able to use and purchase. As you are making your way through the phases of your life, think about who you are now, who you want to be, and what you may need to do to get there. Part of trusting the process and your journey should involve having dreams and goals of who you want to be when you're ready to fly.

As you finish reading this book, I encourage you to think about some goals you may want to accomplish in the next one to two years. Write those goals down somewhere that you can look at every day. At the end of each week and month, reflect on the progress you've made toward those goals. Then do the same at the end of each year. Use this Butterfly Code Framework to assess which phase you are in along your journey. Thinking about your goals and reading and writing about them daily keep them at the top of your mind at all times. You see them, you speak about them, and you write about them. You'll be amazed how your life will start to blossom, and you will start seeing those goals and dreams become reality. Eventually, you will one day be flying yourself, and I hope I've given you enough inspiration to evolve, transform, emerge, and take flight.

CLOSING

As I write the last pages of this book, I'm reflecting on my journey. I just celebrated my forty-ninth birthday, and I feel amazing. While some people dread turning fifty, I'm looking forward to what the next book will be. I'm not calling it the next chapter on purpose. I'm looking forward to living out the rest of this year as the last in my forties and starting my fifties soaring.

I wrote a version of my story between 2009 and 2011 while I was going through my divorce and a very painful period in my life. It was my therapy. Reading and writing have always been something very therapeutic for me. It always created a space for me to escape either in someone else's words or my own. Since my childhood, I've always said I would one day be an author, but I wasn't sure what kind of story I would write. So when I wrote my first book, I knew I would never publish it. I always felt like it was the prologue of what was to come. Those who knew I was writing it or continued to watch my life story change continuously asked when my book was coming out. I was constantly told that I had a story to tell and I should write it. But I knew my story was still unfolding, and it was hard to explain to people that they had to be patient while I was trusting my own process.

This book is over ten years in the making. Some of it has been in my head, and some of it has been in my heart, while a portion of it was on these pages. You see, this book is almost its own version of a butterfly. While my life was going through the stages, it was as well. Now, it's ready to emerge and take flight. I feel extremely honored and proud to share my journey with you, and I'm thankful to those who have encouraged me to keep going. I hope this book inspires you to do the same.

As I close, I'm resting my wings. There is still so much work to do on this journey. There are still so many things I want and need to accomplish, and my story will still continue to evolve, and my life will continue to transform. That's the next book that I'm looking forward to.

ABOUT THE AUTHOR

D'Yanna Craighead is a speaker, transformation coach, author, and an award winning senior technology manager with over 25 years of experience at various large corporations. With a background mixed with software engineering, technical product management, and technical program management she has spent her career delivering large, highly visible technology products around the world.

D'Yanna's biggest passion is inspiring others. As a Black woman in technology, she is an advocate for women and underrepresented communities in technology and can often be found on panels or speaking engagements at various women in technology conferences.

In 2022, D'Yanna created YARA SKY LLC as a platform to provide mentorship and career consulting to women and underrepresented groups using her Butterfly Code Framework through speaking engagements and workshops. Her products for The Butterfly Code Framework, such as guided journals, notebooks, workshops and speaking engagement requests can be found on her website www.thebutterflycode.com.

You can also find out more about D'Yanna at www.dyannacraighead.com or follow her on LinkedIn, Instagram, TikTok, or YouTube.